PERSONNEL FOR THE NEW DIPLOMACY

THE COMMITTEE ON FOREIGN AFFAIRS PERSONNEL

Members

Chairman
THE HONORABLE CHRISTIAN A. HERTER

Vice-Chairman
DON K. PRICE Dean, Graduate School of Public Administration, Harvard University

GEORGE V. ALLEN President, Tobacco Institute, Inc.
KENNETH B. CLARK Professor of Psychology, City College of New York
CARLISLE H. HUMELSINE President, Colonial Williamsburg, Inc.
JOSEPH E. JOHNSON President, Carnegie Endowment for International Peace
MILTON KATZ Director of International Legal Studies, Harvard Law School
JAMES A. PERKINS Vice President, Carnegie Corporation of New York
JAMES ROWE Attorney
JAMES HOPKINS SMITH, JR.
ARTHUR K. WATSON President, IBM World Trade Corporation
JOHN HAY WHITNEY Publisher of New York *Herald Tribune*

Staff of the Committee

Staff Director
FREDERICK C. MOSHER Professor, University of California, Berkeley

Associate Staff Director
ARTHUR G. JONES Foreign Service Officer

Professional Staff:

Gerald W. Bush
Barry Casper
Frances Fielder
John E. Harr
Roene B. Horgan
Fordyce W. Luikart
Nathan Maccoby
R. Kenneth Oakley
Everett W. Reimer

Consultants:

Bertha W. Beaton
Robert E. Elder
Douglas V. LePan
Arthur W. Macmahon
William P. Maddox
Wallace S. Sayre
Arthur G. Stevens
Edward W. Weidner

REPORT OF
THE COMMITTEE ON FOREIGN AFFAIRS PERSONNEL

PERSONNEL
FOR THE NEW
DIPLOMACY

DECEMBER 1962

Published by and under the auspices of the Carnegie Endowment for International Peace on behalf of the Committee on Foreign Affairs Personnel, Washington, D.C., December 1962.

Library of Congress Catalog Card No. 62-22365
Typographic design: Hubert Leckie
Press of Judd & Detweiler, Inc.

FOREWORD

THE WISDOM with which our foreign policies are framed and the skill with which they are carried out depend upon the men and women who conduct our foreign affairs day by day. That they perform well is vital, for upon them rests the welfare, progress, even survival, of our people and, to a high degree, that of the peoples of the free world. In no other field is it more urgent that our Government attract and develop the ablest public servants.

The Committee on Foreign Affairs Personnel was constituted late in 1961 at the request of Secretary of State Rusk. It was established under the auspices of the Carnegie Endowment for International Peace and with financial support provided also by the Ford Foundation and the Rockefeller Brothers Fund. The Committee is composed entirely of private citizens, most of whom have previously been professionally involved in foreign affairs. Its study has been completely independent and impartial.

The Committee has focused its attention on the personnel problems and needs of the Department of State, including the Agency for International Development, and the United States Information Agency. It has inquired into the overseas activities and personnel arrangements used by other Government agencies only to the extent that they were considered relevant to its central task. The Committee did not attempt to deal with the Department of Defense, the Central Intelligence Agency, the United States Arms Control and Disarmament Agency, or the Peace Corps. Under its terms of reference, the Committee could not give these and other elements of our national machinery for foreign affairs the careful study they warrant.

The Committee has concentrated on executive and professional personnel in foreign affairs, in the belief that requirements in these categories are the most crucial. In formulating its proposals, the Committee has focused more on principles than on matters of procedure. In order to view personnel problems in their total context, the Committee has found it necessary to study the role of the Secretary of State and the Department of State, under the President, in the total administration of United States foreign affairs and the relationship between policy formulation, program development, and the human resources required to carry out policies and programs.

The Committee and staff have used various methods of study to increase their understanding of present problems and practices and have drawn on the experience and thinking of those within the services and others intimately familiar with them. A number of key officials appeared before the full Committee.* All employees of the three principal agencies concerned were invited to send in ideas and suggestions. More than one thousand persons were interviewed or participated in group discussions. Committee and staff members visited thirty-two overseas posts scattered in each major region of the world. The staff and consultants conducted a variety of research studies, statistical analyses, inquiries by questionnaire, and brief investigations of certain other foreign services.

The continuing conduct of our foreign affairs will inevitably give rise to new personnel requirements and call for shifts in emphasis and approach. In many respects, we must organize for constant innovation and change. In other respects, we are passing through a period of consolidation, building on values and principles which, in their fundamental aspects, have come to enjoy widespread public support and acceptance. The time is propitious for charting a course of action that can be followed in the decade ahead.

The administration and personnel of the various foreign affairs agencies have been subjected to repeated study over the last twenty years. They have been the butt of sharp criticism, much of it unsubstantiated and undeserved. The Committee is convinced that the

---

* These persons are listed in Appendix A, V.

vast majority of the men and women who make up these agencies are extremely devoted and able public servants; they should be a source of pride to the American people. A report of this kind necessarily probes for areas of weakness and opportunities for improvement. It understates the strengths. The considerable success that has attended many of the efforts of the United States in foreign affairs is in no small degree due to the dedicated persons who have staffed the foreign affairs agencies. The continuing self-criticism and internal renovation of these agencies testify to the constructive spirit of their leadership. Indeed, the formation of the present committee is an example of this forward-looking attitude, and many of the proposals contained in the following report are variants or projections of steps already under way or under consideration in the agencies.

But the problems, the complexities, that will continue to confront us will demand something better than the best of the past. An informed citizen of another country put the issue this way: "The United States now has the best mission it has ever had in my country. It is by far the strongest of all the foreign missions here. I am not sure, however, whether it is good enough." Clearly, the demands are high, and indeed without precedent; the stakes are tremendous.

Our aim is that the recommendations which follow will help make those engaged in foreign affairs at least "good enough," and hopefully a good deal better than that.

Christian A. Herter
Chairman

Don K. Price
Vice-Chairman

Geo. V. Allen

James G. Perkins

Carlisle H. Humelsine

James Rowe

Kenneth B. Clark

H. Smith Jr.

Joseph E. Johnson

Arthur K. Watson

Milton Eisenhower

John Hay Whitney

vii

ACKNOWLEDGMENTS

THE COMMITTEE WISHES TO RECORD its deep appreciation for the invaluable work of its staff. We were very fortunate in having an excellent Staff Director in the person of Dr. Frederick C. Mosher. Dr. Mosher was granted a year's leave of absence from his post as Professor of Political Science, University of California at Berkeley, to work with the Committee. We also had the good fortune to obtain, as Associate Staff Director, Mr. Arthur G. Jones, a Foreign Service Officer who was released to the Committee on loan and who, in his devoted and objective work, typifies the Service at its best. Dr. Mosher and Mr. Jones assembled a small, highly competent group of full-time professional staff members and part-time consultants without whose informed and diligent labors this report could not have been written. Thanks are due also for the special assistance provided by editorial consultant Patricia Wohlgemuth, statistician Robert L. Goldstone, and the secretarial staff: Eloise Baute, Patricia Chatelaine, Madeleine Doty, Georgia Jampalis, Carole Lund, and Nancy McCullough.

The Committee is deeply appreciative of the cooperation and helpfulness with which its inquiries, sometimes troublesome and inconvenient, have been received. The Government agencies and officials concerned, at home and abroad, have been generous with their time and informative assistance. A special note of thanks is due the Department of State, the Agency for International Development, the Federal Aviation Agency, and the Department of the Navy for making available members of their staffs to serve on the Committee's professional staff. The Committee also wishes to express its thanks to George Washington University for making available office space and other services.

CONTENTS

THE DIMENSIONS

OF THE

NEW DIPLOMACY

I

"For our Nation is commissioned by history to be either an observer of freedom's failure or the cause of its success." JOHN F. KENNEDY

THE PRACTICE OF DIPLOMACY between states is among the most ancient and honored institutions of civilized societies. Its maturation among the nations of Europe in the nineteenth century was a significant achievement. It provided, and still provides, the principal mechanism whereby sovereign states can communicate with one another and settle their differences short of war. The European system was the model for the diplomacy of the United States and for the other nations of the world, and European diplomatic services influenced the evolution of the United States service.

However effective this diplomatic model was in years gone by, it is clear that the old system, though still useful and even essential in its central elements, is inadequate by itself for the United States of today. The reasons for this are many, and most of them derive from changes in societies and relationships among peoples that could hardly have been foreseen even a quarter of a century ago. A second and accompanying category of changes stems from the revolutionized role of the United States in world affairs. Behind both these types of change are the enormous and still accelerating technological and scientific developments of recent decades.

1

THE WORLD SETTING

The characteristics of the revolution in international affairs in the past quarter-century are generally well known, but their significance in terms of the staffing of the United States' foreign affairs agencies is not as fully appreciated. It is necessary, therefore, to recall some of these factors in order to point out their impact on our foreign affairs personnel systems.

The most obvious, pervasive, and crucial element in the world situation today is the conflict between the free countries, struggling to build a world of free, independent, peaceful, and progressive peoples, and the Communist world. While the United States and other nations in the past opposed and periodically warred against absolutism in one form or another, never before, short of all-out hostilities, have international energies been so mobilized and so committed to a struggle of this kind. This struggle motivates many international activities, and it colors virtually everything that is done in world affairs. Furthermore, with the quickening pace of incidents at various points in the world and the danger of their rapid escalation to world crises, the critical nature of decisions in foreign affairs has become truly awesome. In no other field of social or political action are the stakes comparable.

A second obvious change has been the shrinkage of the world in terms of the relations among states and between any given state and its emissaries abroad. There is today an immediacy in foreign affairs and a demand for speed of decision and action unknown in the past. International communication can be virtually instantaneous, international travel extremely rapid. Direct conversation between heads of states has become a frequent part of diplomatic machinery.* American citizens are made particularly aware of this immediacy by the presence of the United Nations at their very doorstep on the east side of Manhattan Island. The machinery of this organization makes possible frequent contacts not only among friendly nations but also between them and others that are non-aligned and even with most of those that are hostile.

An accompanying factor is the interlocking of states and of conflicting or parallel interests all around the world. Disturbances in Laos or Berlin or Cuba may touch off diplomatic problems thousands of miles away. Keeping up with developments and correlating them with policies and programs in a consistent manner have become problems of the greatest complexity.

---

* In the first year and three-quarters of the Kennedy Administration, for example, more than fifty chiefs of state or heads of government visited Washington.

A fourth element of change in diplomacy has arisen from the need to deal with *peoples* of nations as well as with their governments. Traditional diplomacy was designed almost exclusively to govern relationships between representatives of heads of states. Today, much foreign activity involves the representation of whole peoples before whole peoples of other societies. This relationship between peoples is most conspicuous in connection with information programs, cultural programs, educational exchanges, trade fairs, and like enterprises. It is equally important in most international development undertakings in which foreign representatives deal not only with government ministries but also with a great variety of institutions, organizations, and individuals in the local society. Even in the more traditional activities of foreign services, a great deal more attention must be paid than formerly to the many forces, factions, and interests on the local scene in addition to the government in power. And in the view of local populations, official representatives, no matter what their function and no matter what agency has sent them, are seen and judged as prototypes, for better or worse, of the nation they represent.

A further dimension of change in the diplomatic area arises from the sudden and dramatic emergence of new states, particularly in Africa and Asia. There are, at this writing, 110 members of the United Nations, and its membership continues to grow. Twenty-five years ago we exchanged ambassadors with only 17 nations, and ministers with 43. Today, there are more than 100 ambassadorial posts.

A most significant source of change in diplomacy today derives from the demands for rapid social, economic, and political progress in so many of these nations, as well as in the older nations of Latin America. No longer can the purpose of diplomacy be confined to a narrow or insular view of national interest. Our diplomacy, as well as that of many other industrialized nations, is now committed to assisting developing countries to achieve their aspirations for growth.

Traditional diplomacy, with its conventions and accepted practices, assumed that relations between states would normally be carried out on a bilateral basis. Today, account must also be taken of a complex of international and regional machinery, most of it created since World War II. In addition to the United Nations itself, there are many permanent international organizations operating in such specialized fields as agriculture, health, banking, investment, communications, and labor. Beyond these are a variety of regional organizations such as the North Atlantic Treaty Organization, the Southeast Asia Treaty Organization, the Organization of American States, the Intergovernmental Committee for European Migration, and others; and there are countless other multilateral arrangements of one or another type—temporary, *ad hoc,* periodic. Indeed, part of the challenge of diplomacy today lies in the invention of new forms and structures of international relations to meet emerging problems.

THE ROLE AND ACTIVITIES OF THE UNITED STATES

The new dimensions cited above have had a particular impact on the United States because of the transformation of this country's role in the affairs of the world. The posture of the United States changed dramatically in the direction of active participation in foreign affairs at the time of the Spanish-American War. The movement toward a more activist policy in foreign affairs has been sporadic rather than consistent but was greatly accelerated as a consequence of both the world wars of this century. By the 1950's there could be no doubt that we had acquired, however gladly or however reluctantly, leading responsibilities among the nations of the free world. Our interest in every part of the world is today extensive, and our commitment to the pursuit of growth and progress among the free nations is well-nigh total.

In pursuit of our international goals, we have developed an arsenal of instruments more varied than ever before. They include: all the tools of traditional diplomacy; international law; intelligence; political action; technical assistance and various types of foreign economic aid; military aid programs; information and psychological programs; monetary policies; trade development programs; educational exchange; cultural programs; and, more recently, measures to counter insurgency movements. Most of these fall outside the older definition of diplomacy, but all of them must be considered actual or potential elements of United States programs. Together they constitute what is here called the "new diplomacy."

With the expansion of our commitment and of our instruments for effectuating foreign policy goals has come an intermingling of foreign affairs considerations with other national objectives and interests. The most dramatic example of this is the connection between foreign affairs policy and military policy, a combination now widely known as national security policy. Not too long ago, our diplomatic and military establishments planned and operated with comparatively little relation or attention one to the other. Diplomacy was presumably predominant until we overpassed the brink of war; then the military agencies took over. Today, many of the most important foreign policy problems are also military problems. Under the President, the foreign affairs and defense agencies must work in continuous concert and with mutual understanding, both in peace and in war.

The fusion of foreign policy considerations with domestic problems is illustrated across the whole range of national interests. Every major department and agency of the national government has an immediate concern in some phase of our foreign policy. Indeed, the distinction between what is foreign and what is domestic is often more confusing than useful. Our relationships with other nations are tied inextricably to our internal growth, our prosperity, our scientific and technological development, and our domestic politics.

With increasing United States commitment abroad, the problems of coordinating, correlating, and administering the overseas programs have become enormous. For example, some 28 Federal agencies employ about 32,000 United States citizens in civilian capacities in some 127 foreign countries, colonies, and dependencies. About 58 per cent of these employees work for the Department of Defense; another 37 per cent are employed by the State Department, the Agency for International Development, and the United States Information Agency; and the remaining 5 per cent are scattered among 20 other Federal departments and agencies. These figures exclude some 95,000 foreign nationals who are also employed by United States agencies abroad.

The complexity can be illustrated in other ways. The United States Government must provide representation in the governing bodies of a growing number of international and regional organizations. It must provide for the participation of United States officials and private citizens in an ever increasing number of international conferences— 474 between July 1, 1961, and June 30, 1962, alone, or an average of almost two new ones starting every workday in the year. Almost 2,800 United States delegates participated.

There is one further aspect of United States diplomacy which represents a substantial departure from the traditional diplomacy of the past. It arises from the remarkable growth of interest in foreign policy among millions of United States citizens and from their legitimate concern about the costs, particularly of defense and foreign aid. Diplomacy today involves more than representation of the United States' interests abroad; it requires, in effect, a continuous representation of foreign policy questions to the people. The increased interest and concern of our people in the conduct of foreign affairs is reflected in the role played by the Congress in the formulation and execution of foreign policy. Under our constitutional form of government, the powers vested in the Congress take on special significance in meeting the demands of the new diplomacy. While the Executive Branch under the President must exercise leadership in the formulation of policies and programs, the Congress not only provides the requisite authorization and appropriations in their support, but may and often does assume the initiative. In short, diplomacy cannot operate in a vacuum at home and our Congressional leaders and responsible officials in the Executive Branch must give attention to the temper of the people at large and to the many groups and organizations that reflect the diversity of our society, including private businesses, labor organizations, the educational world, and a host of other public and private groups.

THE NEW DIPLOMATS

The basic and rapid changes in the nature of the world and in the role of the United States have clearly called into being a new and an enlarged concept of foreign affairs, and this in turn entails a different conception of the role and the kinds of personnel engaged in it. In this report, the Committee offers a number of recommendations directed to equipping our foreign affairs personnel better to handle the problems of the new diplomacy. Principal among the objectives are the following three:

First, it is apparent that our foreign policy goals cannot be pursued in a posture of passivity—of observing and reporting. To be sure, there is as great a stake as ever in accurate, perceptive, up-to-date information about developments in other countries, and the Committee would certainly not condone any slighting of the reportorial functions. But all of the foreign affairs agencies are heavily involved in operations, in *doing* things overseas. Their responsibilities include not only watching things happen and reporting them, but also helping to make them happen or at least influencing their happening. We have an overriding need to utilize the instruments available to us in ways that will help give a positive and constructive orientation to the forces of change. Our personnel systems must be adapted to recruiting and developing officers oriented to, and capable of, this kind of performance.

Equally clearly, the responsibilities of this country in world affairs cannot be adequately met by "generalists" with a superficial knowledge of all relevant specialties. Quality is required, as it always has been, but today the need is for quality in many different areas and many different professions. Our personnel systems must be adapted to recruiting and developing and utilizing a growing diversity in talents and skills.

Finally, our representatives overseas are not merely representatives of the individual agencies that sent them there or of their particular specialties or professions. They are first and foremost representatives of the United States. It is therefore essential that there be an underlying level of understanding and agreement among foreign

6

affairs officials as to the goals of our nation and our democratic system. These officials should also understand and agree on the content and use of the various possible instruments in achieving those goals. The very diversity of skills and knowledges mentioned above makes more necessary, and also more difficult, a common appreciation of national purpose. Such an appreciation must be built on a foundation of knowledge of the circumstances in which we operate, the tools we may employ, and the relations of those tools one to the other. There is always a danger, in large and complex enterprises, of compartmentation, divisiveness, jealousy, and parochialism. In the chapters that follow, the Committee proposes measures to achieve a greater degree of unity amid the diversity of talents, perspectives, and efforts required in foreign affairs. This is merely another way of stating the national motto, which has both described and served the United States so very well for so very long. The personnel systems in foreign affairs should be so conceived as to contribute both to the diversity and to the unity.

POLITICAL LEADERSHIP AND CAREERS

In the field of foreign affairs, the President, the Secretary of State, and other high officials carry a fearful burden of responsibility for prompt and courageous decisions which are the more difficult for being essentially irreversible. Political leadership alone, however, cannot cope unaided with the complexities of foreign affairs. It must be undergirded by professional career services whose members, drawn from all segments of society, are well grounded in their understanding of, and capacity to use, the instruments of the new diplomacy.

The use of career public servants in filling top executive posts raises an important issue of public policy which the Committee believes merits special comment. The Committee takes it as self-evident that the President must and will have freedom to choose from the entire national pool of qualified men and women in selecting key appointive officials in foreign affairs. Career officers should constitute a prime resource within the national pool. They should receive no less consideration than others as potential choices for the highest executive posts; they should neither enjoy an automatic priority nor suffer from an adverse presumption. Rather they should be deemed available and encouraged to aspire to such posts with the knowledge that they will be appraised in competition with others drawn from any part of the nation's human resources. They can ask or expect no more. If the quality, training, and experience of career officers are steadily upgraded as recommended in this report, increasing numbers of them are bound to be selected for high executive posts at home as well as abroad.

This concept is consistent with, and does no violence to, the principle of Presidential control. Political direction must, of course, emanate from the President, but political direction need not conflict with the need for depth of experience in, and professional knowledge of, foreign affairs, whether acquired within or outside the career services. Whoever is appointed to positions of top executive responsibility must enjoy the confidence of the responsible political head—the President, the Secretary of State, or heads of other foreign affairs agencies, as the case may be. Those so appointed must also be prepared to accept the political hazards implicit in these positions.

* * * * *

The Committee is impressed, as all Americans should be, by the long strides our foreign affairs establishment has already taken in adjusting to, and even in pioneering, the new diplomacy. Our capacity to respond to changed situations improves year by year. Only in part is the new diplomacy a goal to be achieved; in many respects, it exists now. It is to the remaining tasks and possible improvements that this report is addressed.

II

LEADERSHIP IN FOREIGN AFFAIRS

"A prerequisite to the achievement of all our international affairs and finance programs is dynamic, positive, and dedicated leadership by the Department of State."

DWIGHT D. EISENHOWER

SUMMARY

For the purpose of making more effective the role of the Secretary of State and the Department of State with regard to all aspects of foreign affairs:

- the Department's role should embrace not only the formulation of foreign policies, but also leadership in seeing that they are effectuated; the capacity of the Department to provide this leadership and coordination in the conduct of foreign affairs needs to be strengthened;
- a new post of Executive Under Secretary of State should be established, subordinate in rank only to the Secretary and Under Secretary, to assure that foreign policies and programs are carried out with maximum effectiveness;
- a programing system should be established whereby policies are translated into plans of action and used as a basis for projecting personnel and other needs in foreign affairs.

UNDER OUR CONSTITUTIONAL SYSTEM, the President and the Congress exercise wide powers in the conduct of foreign relations. The sheer range and complexity of foreign policy problems dictate the need

9

for a central staff arm of the President to exert leadership both in the formulation and execution of foreign policy. The Committee emphatically endorses the view that the Department of State, under the Secretary of State, should provide this leadership—in Washington, in each country abroad, and in international organizations.

The Department of State has concentrated primarily on formulating and coordinating foreign policy. It has not developed adequately either the attitudes or the machinery needed to relate policies to the operations required to carry them out. This is true both with respect to the Department's role in the Executive Branch as a whole, and with respect to its own internal activities. The traditional concept of the Foreign Service diplomat has not fostered what might be called a "programing sense." There has been some disposition, reflected in organizational shifts in the not too distant past, to divorce the Department from "operations" so that it could engage exclusively in policy matters. Such a divorce, never consistently sought or fully effected, is clearly not feasible in today's context.

The Committee is convinced that the Department's capacity to assist the President in coordinating the programs and operations of the entire Federal Government in the field of foreign affairs must be strengthened. Likewise, the tendency within the Department to view what is called "administration" as separate, subordinate, and of little relevance to the foreign policy function must be corrected. The recommendations in this chapter, which are intended to achieve these goals, go somewhat beyond the personnel field, strictly defined, but they constitute an indispensable starting point. Indeed, some of the most significant personnel recommendations in this report will remain pious hopes unless steps are taken in these directions.

STRENGTHENING THE DEPARTMENT OF STATE
Recommendation 1

The capacity of the Department of State to assist the President in providing leadership and coordination in foreign affairs must be strengthened. The Department's responsibility should embrace the formulation of foreign policy, the development and coordination of foreign affairs programs, and the planning and marshaling of the resources needed for their implementation.

Whatever the Department of State does in exercising leadership and coordination, it must do as an agent of the President. It follows that the Department must have the confidence and support of the President. If the Department's leadership role is to be clearly established and recognized by the many Government departments and agencies involved in foreign policy or operations, then, manifestly, its professional service must be equipped to respond to the needs of the new diplomacy and to make effective innovations desired by the President and the Secretary of State. The Department should ensure that foreign policy objectives are translated into programs of action, that these programs are coordinated and adjusted in the light of changing needs, and that an effective union is achieved between policies and programs, on the one hand, and their administration, on the other. Its mission should encompass the forward planning and utilization of the personnel and other resources needed to do the job. Despite the enormous demands already made upon his time and stamina, the Secretary must regard these as among his principal responsibilities and inseparable from those of formulating foreign policy and conducting day-to-day diplomatic negotiations.

A NEW POST OF EXECUTIVE UNDER SECRETARY OF STATE *

Recommendation 2

A new post of Executive Under Secretary, subordinate in rank only to the Secretary and Under Secretary, should be established in the Department of State. The Executive Under Secretary should act in the Secretary's behalf in assuring that:

(a) foreign affairs personnel and machinery are adequate to the nation's international responsibilities;

(b) policies are supported by action programs and by the means and resources for their realization;

(c) the processes of policymaking, program development, budgeting, and administration are brought into an effective union; and

(d) interagency relationships and personnel arrangements are properly coordinated.

The fusion in the Secretary of State of enormous political, advisory, representational, and managerial responsibilities makes his a nearly impossible task. The Under Secretary is as pressed as the Secretary by immediate problems on the international scene. He acts as an *alter ego* to the Secretary, and frequently serves as Acting Secretary. Neither man can give continuous attention to the management of programs and activities of the Department of State and to their co-

---

* A dissenting opinion to this section and to Recommendation 2 by Messrs. George V. Allen and James Rowe appears on pp. 15-18.

ordination with the programs of other Government agencies engaged in foreign affairs. For this there must be another officer at a high level of authority and prestige. The Committee therefore proposes the creation of the statutory position of Executive Under Secretary of State, the occupant of which would be subordinate within the Department's structure only to the Secretary and Under Secretary.

The Executive Under Secretary's primary responsibility should be to make sure that the resources of the Department of State and the other principal foreign affairs agencies are giving maximum support to the Secretary of State in his role as leader and coordinator, under the President, of the foreign relations of the United States. This responsibility would require him to keep in close touch with the Congress and the various departments and agencies of the Government. Acting as a senior staff officer, he would take the lead in arranging for cooperative action on those matters that no one officer can be given full power to administer. He should provide leadership in bringing about the personnel arrangements recommended in this report. This task alone would be sufficient reason for strengthening the top-level structure of the State Department.

The Executive Under Secretary should participate in the preparation of new or modified policies and programs. He should act for the Secretary in seeing that policies are translated into coordinated programs of action and that program plans are supported by adequate institutional resources such as funds, personnel, organization and methods, and communications and other logistical support.

The Committee wishes to emphasize its conviction that the Executive Under Secretary should command a range of responsibilities broader than the internal administration of the State Department. He should bring to bear the resources of the several departments and agencies of the Government concerned with foreign affairs in order to achieve the objectives of our foreign policy. He should play a central role in the orderly programing of the operations of the foreign affairs agencies and their translation into personnel and budgetary terms. He should assure that the budgets and personnel policies and programs of the principal foreign affairs agencies are in harmony and consistent with the over-all foreign policy objectives of the United States.

Responsibility within the Department of State for the important functions of internal organizational planning, budget and fiscal management, central personnel management and training, inspection and evaluation, and a multitude of supporting administrative services is now centered in the Deputy Under Secretary for Administration and the Assistant Secretary for Administration. These two posts should be consolidated under either title. This officer would be directly responsible for the internal administration of the Department of State, under the Executive Under Secretary. This task in itself is formidable. The Department—including its Foreign Service proper but leaving aside the Agency for International Development, the United States Arms Control and Disarmament Agency, and the Peace Corps—employs almost 24,000 persons embracing a wide range of specialities. Its overseas staff of 6,700 United States citizens and 10,000 local employees is dispersed throughout the world at some 282 embassies, legations, special missions, and consular offices.

The position of the Executive Under Secretary should be filled by a person who enjoys the full confidence of the President and the Secretary of State. He should be knowledgeable in foreign affairs, preferably on the basis of extensive overseas service, and should be experienced in the workings of the legislative and administrative processes in Washington. The President and the Secretary should, of course, be free to choose for this position the most qualified person, whatever his background. But the Committee recommends that the post normally be filled by a career public official or by a person with pertinent experience in the public service; if the personnel systems are strengthened as this report proposes, it should seldom be necessary to turn elsewhere for lack of career talent. The Committee would expect that the persons appointed to this position would remain in the job for extended periods of time and thus provide much-needed continuity of experience.

PROGRAMING FOREIGN AFFAIRS ACTIVITIES
Recommendation 3

Under the leadership of the Executive Under Secretary of State, a system should be established whereby foreign policy objectives are translated into programs of action to be undertaken in each area of foreign affairs activity, projected as far into the future as is feasible, and used as a basis for estimating future personnel and other needs in foreign affairs.

The State Department pays insufficient attention to the translation of policies into action programs. Many policy statements prepared within the Department are so general that they provide only vague guidance for the development of operating programs and administrative plans. Some of these documents have borne about the same relationship to program plans as the Constitution of the United States bears to the annual budget. (Under the aegis of the Policy

Planning Council in the State Department, work is now under way to develop far more specific statements of plans and objectives in relation to selected foreign countries. These should be very useful to regional, country-desk, and other officials of the foreign affairs agencies for the development of operating programs.)

Furthermore, there is no central machinery or procedure in the State Department either to coordinate foreign affairs program planning or to use program plans as a basis for estimates of immediate and longer-range personnel needs. In the absence of such machinery, statements of personnel requirements have been the products of annual budgets, which in turn have been framed largely within arbitrary ceilings on the basis of historical rather than future needs. Budget administration and personnel management under such circumstances are largely a matter of extinguishing fires, often at the expense of other needs of a lower order of emergency but higher importance.

The United States Information Agency and the Agency for International Development give considerably more attention to program planning—that is, to determining the nature, scope, and timing of specific actions to be taken in order to achieve stated objectives. This is not surprising since these agencies, more than the Department of State, are concerned essentially with operations. Neither agency, however, has yet developed effective means for translating program plans into long-term projections of personnel needs.

The Department of State should provide leadership in the development and continuous supervision of a programing system that will integrate policy formulation, program development, and administration in foreign affairs. In accordance with Recommendation 2, responsibility for leadership, coordination, supervision, and follow-up should be taken by the proposed Executive Under Secretary, acting in behalf of the Secretary of State. This responsibility is the most important to be entrusted to this new office.

Each foreign affairs agency, including the State Department itself, should establish suitable internal machinery for programing its own activities within a broader framework provided by the Executive Under Secretary of State. Whatever organizational arrangements are utilized for generating programs, a central point within each agency is needed to coordinate program planning and translate program designs into manpower, financial, and other logistical requirements. Annual budgets should be an outgrowth and refined expression of such programs and administrative plans. They should take into account not only next year's requirements, but also the cost of preparing for subsequent years. Projected manpower requirements should be translated into plans for immediate operations in the personnel field, including recruitment and selection, career development, training, and so forth. This latter aspect of programing is discussed in Chapter V.

The programing system should include provision for periodic appraisal of programs and for making modifications in the light of experience and new developments. A five- to ten-year projection of needs should be reappraised at least annually and adjusted accordingly. The Executive Under Secretary and his immediate staff should work closely with each agency in all phases of the programing cycle.

Dissent By George V. Allen and James Rowe

PERMANENT UNDER SECRETARY

We have no quarrel with the reasoning which underlies the recommendation by the Majority of this Committee of the position of Executive Under Secretary.

We would argue, however, that the solution proposed does not go far enough.

We recommend instead creation of the post of "Permanent Under Secretary," *deliberately* and *symbolically* so named, to be filled, by nomination of the President with the advice and consent of the Senate, from the top echelon of the Foreign Service. This post, the highest to which a career officer would aspire, would be the third-ranking post in the Department.

The Permanent Under Secretary—unlike the proposed "Executive Under Secretary" of the Majority—would be in the direct chain of command over the Under Secretary for Political Affairs, the Under Secretary for Economic Affairs, and the regional and functional Assistant Secretaries on foreign policy problems. If he is not in such chain of command his duties are likely to be generally the same as, and no more than, those of the present Deputy Under Secretary for Administration. He would, of course, be in the direct chain of command over the Deputy Under Secretary for Administration.

It is a commonplace that the Department of State does not function today, and has not functioned for many years, in an efficient fashion at either the policymaking level or the management level. The device suggested here simply and symbolically places the day-to-day policy operating control of the Department in all its facets in the third position in the Department. Much more important, it would emphasize continuity of policy by the selection of a career Foreign Service Officer, a "nonpolitical animal," to fill the position.

The time has come to recognize that the Department of State is in this modern world an entirely different institution from the other departments and agencies in our governmental structure. The problems with which it deals are so complex that it should no longer be regarded as subject to the same black-and-white rules of public administration that may apply to those other departments and agencies.

The political scientists insist that every department should be subject to political control at the top. With a change in administrations, the old guard gives way to the new. This is sound doctrine.

But however one approaches the Department of State—whether from the point of view of the organization and improvement of its personnel, as has this Committee, or from the point of view of the making and execution of foreign policy, as many other studies have—one thing is clear:

Because of the complexity of foreign policy problems and programs, there must be, from administration to administration—and at the very top of the governmental structure—a *continuity* of knowledge, of management, of administration. In almost all cases and almost all situations this continuity of policy and of management should and must flow consistently, irrespective of domestic political change.

In the precise sense the function of the Permanent Under Secretary would be to "manage" the Department, using the word "manage" in all its definitions. He would be immersed in the making of diplomatic policy as, indeed, he has been throughout his career. He would be immersed as a top-flight executive, in managing the personnel and budgetary problems of the Department.

Essentially, his duty would be to turn policies into programs.

The final decisions of policy and of management would be made by him subject only to the orders, modifications, or reversals of the Secretary and the Under Secretary, the political officers selected by the President to advise him and to carry out his foreign policy.

There may have been a time in American history, and there probably was, when very bright men could come into the higher echelons of the Department of State, rather quickly absorb and understand the problems of the day, and make almost immediately a real contribution to the Department, the President, and the nation. They would return after a year or two of public service to private life with a real sense of having done a thorough and competent job.

Hardly anyone believes that can any longer be true. For some reason this apparently is understood far better when it is discussed in relation to the Department of Defense. There the position of Chairman of the Joint Chiefs of Staff is roughly equivalent, in authority and responsibility, to the position recommended here of Permanent Under Secretary in the Department of State.

Certainly today's military problems are complex and infinitely difficult but, almost by definition, they must be less difficult and less complex, and certainly less intangible than those of foreign policy, of which military policy is only a part.

A lifetime of experience in the intricate art of making foreign policy and executing programs would seem to be the only real preparation for this position of top management. Certainly any other profession, such as the law or business or banking, or any other discipline such as teaching in a large university, is at best an inadequate substitute.

It has been suggested that the third-ranking officer who "manages" the Department cannot be in the direct chain of command over the Assistant Secretaries on policy problems since he would become a "bottleneck" between them and the Secretary. The simple answer is that an instinctively good administrator never allows himself to become such a bottleneck. In any event, this position will always require a remarkable man. There will be little place anywhere in the future of this Department for unremarkable men.

The President will still have adequate political control, when he wishes to exercise it, through the Secretary or the Under Secretary. But post-World War II experience has shown that these two men are always almost wholly absorbed in the top ten or twelve priority problems at most, and cannot, in terms either of time or of energy, really devote themselves to the day-to-day management of the Department, including the myriad problems on foreign policy that are not temporarily important enough to find their way to the top of the priority list.

Whatever it may be worth, the British and French Foreign Services, in departments infinitely smaller than our Department of State, have long had such a post as Permanent Under Secretary, always staffed by a career officer who functions in the manner suggested here.

This post, as outlined, would do away with the pretense that there is in government a real difference in practice between policy and administration. No governmental department except the Department of State has ever attempted to function in such an unreal manner. Many of the glaring failures of the Department as an institution today can be laid at the door of its real effort to divide policy and administration.

It is useful to add a word of clarification. While the Permanent Under Secretary would be a career Foreign Service Officer, he would have no right to permanent tenure. He could be changed, at the will or even at the whim, if one wishes, of the President and the Secretary. Indeed, it might well be desirable for incoming administrations to make such a change within the first year.

Probably there would be approximately twenty men from whom the President, with the recommendation of the Secretary, might make a selection. A Secretary displeased with his first selection could recommend another career Foreign Service Officer. It is contemplated that the displaced Permanent Under Secretary, if he desires, could return to the field as an Ambassador. The Assistant Secretaries could, in large measure, be appointments from outside the Service, as they often are now. Career Foreign Service Officers would not be precluded from filling such positions but would not be entitled to them as a matter of right or tradition.

It may be felt the President's right to appoint would be too restricted by rigid selection from a too narrow field. Yet his power of appointment is often restricted in the government to a select and trained group. No one ever suggests a military Chief of Staff be a civilian. Here, as there, a top professional with lifetime experience and training is the desirable goal.

The principal argument against the requirement that the Permanent Under Secretary be a Career Officer is this restriction of Presidential choice in appointments. We would agree if a tradition of career appointments existed in the United States as it does in the Foreign Offices of most other countries, or if, as in the appointments to the Joint Chiefs of Staff, the choice of career men were so self-evident. To institute this practice in the Department of State we believe the appointment of a Foreign Service career officer should be specified.

Presidential political control will still exist. But something new and equally important, the continuity of flow of policy, of information, of knowledge, and of experienced management, will have been added.

A FRAMEWORK FOR FOREIGN AFFAIRS PERSONNEL MANAGEMENT

"No nation can maintain greatness for an extended period of time unless its ever-changing political superstructure is supported by an enduring framework of competent devoted public servants."
LOY W. HENDERSON

SUMMARY

In order to provide a rational personnel framework for the conduct of foreign affairs activities at home and abroad:

- career foreign services should be established for the permanent professional personnel of the foreign information and foreign aid programs;
- under the leadership of the Executive Under Secretary of State, the respective foreign affairs personnel systems of the Department of State, USIA, and AID should be organized and administered as a family of compatible systems reflecting substantial uniformity in personnel policies and coordinated personnel operations; each agency should, however, retain administrative control of personnel actions involving its employees;
- the domestic as well as the overseas personnel of the Department of State, USIA, and AID should be administered outside the Civil Service system under arrangements that will provide each agency head maximum flexibility in the use of his personnel and will assure equitable treatment of all personnel;
- each foreign affairs agency should have its own service, distinctively identified, within which personnel should be grouped

in appropriate categories; but all personnel should be paid on the basis of a single salary schedule;
- the Foreign Service of the United States should, as a general rule, serve as the vehicle for activities of the primarily domestic agencies of the Government which have an important bearing on foreign policy; for this purpose, its personnel administration should be modified to accommodate better the needs and interests of those agencies.

WERE IT POSSIBLE to photograph the foreign affairs personnel systems of United States Government agencies, the resulting picture would resemble a patchwork quilt. New and hasty improvisations mix uneasily with old and well-established practices.

Each organization in the foreign affairs field is to a degree unique. Each of the three major agencies—the State Department, the United States Information Agency, and the Agency for International Development—is required to operate under two distinctly different systems, with Civil Service employees bulking large at home and foreign service employees overseas. Other departments and agencies with overseas interests and activities likewise have varied systems. For example, the Departments of Agriculture and Treasury have their own foreign services, administered under the Civil Service system. The Departments of Commerce and Labor look to the Foreign Service of the State Department for commercial and labor services abroad.

Officers and boards within the agencies, the agency heads, the Secretary of State, the Civil Service Commission, the Bureau of the Budget, the White House, other Government departments, and a number of different Congressional committees and subcommittees all have, at one time or another, an important voice in certain personnel decisions. The locus of responsibility and authority varies widely from system to system. To take just one example: Foreign Service Officers are appointed and promoted by the President subject to Senate confirmation; their counterparts in USIA and AID are appointed and promoted by the agency head.

One of the more stable elements in this situation has been the Foreign Service of the United States, as it has been called since 1924. Its history ranges back to the days of the founding fathers. The modern Foreign Service, however, dates from the Rogers Act of 1924, which consolidated the diplomatic and consular services under a single roof. This Act laid the groundwork for the establishment of a professional career corps safeguarded from political patronage and selected in the main by competitive examination for appointment at the bottom class.

The Foreign Service Act of 1946, designed to improve and

strengthen the Service, retained the basic concept of a disciplined and mobile corps. It also established the Foreign Service Reserve, whereby qualified persons from Government or private life could be brought in for temporary periods to supplement the skills not otherwise available within the professional career service, and the Foreign Service Staff category as a corps of clerical, administrative, and technical support personnel. The 1946 Act encouraged a broadened recruitment base, provided more attractive salaries and benefits, contemplated more rapid advancement of able men and the separation of men who had reached their ceilings of performance, and provided that Foreign Service Officers serve a minimum period in the United States. It also created the Foreign Service Institute to provide a continuous program of in-service training.

The Foreign Service Officer Corps is today regarded as the instrument for staffing a variety of professional work at home and abroad. Its functions overseas fall broadly into five categories—executive direction, political, economic, and consular affairs, and administration. When assigned to Washington, Foreign Service Officers staff such other functions as intelligence research, international organization affairs, and public and cultural affairs. On the theory that they must represent the Government of the United States to officials of the countries to which they will be accredited, all Foreign Service Officers are commissioned by the President as diplomatic or consular agents at the time of their appointment; some officers, however, particularly those engaged in administrative work, do not in fact deal with foreign officials in a diplomatic or consular sense. Attachés (commercial, labor, and so forth), while they are often Foreign Service Officers and therefore given Presidential commissions, are simply given this non-commissioned designation by the Secretary of State. Attachés are, in effect, attached to the diplomatic mission and, by international custom, are given full diplomatic privileges.

But the Foreign Service of the United States is not the only foreign service. AID and USIA each have distinct foreign services, though neither has been authorized to establish a career system analogous to that of Foreign Service Officers—long a source of difficulties within those agencies and also in their relationship with the State Department. Furthermore, the major agencies utilize foreign service employees in domestic jobs—in the State Department more than a thousand are posted to Washington—thus magnifying the problems inherent in dual personnel administration.

Variety in personnel systems has certain virtues, especially where it permits flexible personnel arrangements adapted to different kinds of needs. But variety built of improvisation and accidents of history often has an opposite effect, limiting executive freedom of action, inhibiting the employment and retention of the highest-quality people, and damaging employee morale. The Committee believes that these effects are discernible in the foreign affairs agencies at present. In this chapter, therefore, it offers a number of recommendations directed to building a more orderly framework for foreign affairs personnel management.

CAREER PERSONNEL SYSTEMS FOR FOREIGN INFORMATION AND DEVELOPMENT PROGRAMS

Recommendation 4

A career foreign service, to be known as the Foreign Information Service, should be provided for the permanent professional personnel in overseas informational and cultural activities.

In 1953, under the President's Reorganization Plan No. 8, the United States Information Agency (USIA) was established as an independent agency outside the Department of State but subject to its foreign policy guidance. This organizational arrangement has proved to be the stablest in the history of overseas informational and cultural programs, the earliest of which began before World War II. For several years after the war, these programs were administered within the Department of State. The mission of the Agency, "to promote the better understanding of the United States among the peoples of the world and to strengthen cooperative international relations," is pursued through a variety of activities. These include, among others, radio broadcasts through the Voice of America, production and provision overseas of motion pictures, publications and press releases, television films and tapes, and operation of information centers, libraries, and cultural centers. The Agency also administers cultural relations and educational exchange programs abroad in behalf of the State Department, which directs these activities in Washington. The Agency operates in about 100 countries overseas—virtually all except those behind the Iron Curtain—as the United States Information Service (USIS); these overseas offices are integral parts of the diplomatic and consular posts; their director in each country is a public affairs officer who is part of the ambassador's "country team."

USIA employs about 11,000 people, of whom the great majority (8,300) are in the Agency's foreign service. Only about 1,600 of these are United States citizens. Its civil service, largely in Washington, numbers some 2,600 employees.*

---

*Data as of June 30, 1962.

The Agency's foreign service is administered under the provisions of the Foreign Service Act of 1946 relevant to the Reserve, Staff, and local employees. It does not directly employ any Foreign Service Officers, although a few work for the Agency on detail from the State Department. Since 1955, the Agency has sought, without success, legislative authority to establish a career service comparable to that of the Foreign Service Officer Corps. Failing this, the Agency has moved as far as it could administratively by establishing a "Career Reserve Officer Corps," which now includes about 800 officers, modeled on the Foreign Service Officer Corps. Each of its members has successfully undergone a qualifying in-service or entry examination. The Agency regularly recruits junior officer candidates and gives them examinations like those for the Foreign Service and on the same days. Its promotion system and many other personnel practices are like those of the Foreign Service Officers, and representatives of the Foreign Service serve on USIA personnel boards and panels.

In certain important respects, however, the career reserve system differs from the career system of the Foreign Service. For example, under present legislative authorization, the Agency cannot employ Reserve officers beyond a ten-year maximum unless it is given annually a special Congressional authorization for a one-year extension in its appropriation bill. Failure to obtain extensions would do irreparable damage to the program, and continued existence of such limitation is not conducive to the building of a secure and stable service. Likewise, the Agency lacks authority to select-out low-performance officers; its foreign service personnel are under the Civil Service rather than the Foreign Service retirement system; and the ceiling on the advancement of highly qualified senior officers is lower than that of Foreign Service Officers, since they are not eligible for promotion above class 1. In spite of these handicaps, USIA has developed a sound personnel system, and the officer corps includes many with long experience in the Agency and its predecessors.

There can now be no question that the information and cultural programs are an enduring and organic tool of American foreign policy. The Committee believes that it is in the national interest to authorize a career system comparable to that of the Foreign Service Officer Corps for the professional personnel in overseas information and cultural activities. Inasmuch as the career reserve officers now in the Agency have already satisfied standards comparable to those required of Foreign Service Officers, this step could be taken quite easily by simple conversion of the career reserve to full career status.

Recommendation 5

A career foreign service, to be known as the Foreign Development Service, should be provided for the core professional personnel of the foreign aid and development programs. This service should be limited to the professional and administrative personnel required for the continuing management of these programs but also adaptable to other foreign affairs work. It should exclude specialized and technical personnel employed on a project basis.

The Agency for International Development (AID) was established on November 3, 1961, as an agency within the Department of State and under the Secretary of State. It is the latest in a succession of organizations charged with the conduct of United States foreign aid programs over the course of the past two decades. These organizations have been variously located within the Executive Branch. From the beginning, they and their personnel have been a continuing object of popular, Congressional, and Executive Branch interest and criticism. Changes in organization, program, and leadership have been frequent. The latest reorganization, begun in 1961, has been prolonged, uneasy, and difficult. It has involved major changes in leadership, organizational structure, policies, programs, and administration. Underlying this there has been a deepening of uncertainties concerning the future scope and magnitude of foreign assistance activities. Unfortunately, the program over the years has suffered from the injection of patronage pressures.

A principal source of difficulty in our foreign aid programs has been the rapid turnover in top leadership of the foreign assistance agencies. In the approximately fifteen years since the establishment of the Economic Cooperation Administration in 1948, the succession of foreign assistance agencies has had no less than ten chief administrators or directors, and eight directors of personnel.* Almost every new agency head brought with him his own ideas as to how the agency should be organized, who his top assistants should be, and what kind of personnel program was needed. Often, the new agency head or his director of personnel instituted major changes in personnel policies and practices before the previous set of changes had had a chance either to prove or disprove itself. Clearly, many of the agencies' weaknesses in personnel and other administrative practices, which have seriously impaired their effectiveness, can be attributed directly to these frequent changes in top leadership. Accordingly, the Committee believes that every effort should be made to introduce

*Even as this report is going to press, the Agency is to receive a new chief administrator, and possibly another change in direction and emphasis.

greater stability at this level than it has had in the past. This will go far in attracting and keeping the high caliber of personnel that the program deserves.

Effective assistance to the developing countries in achieving free and orderly growth has become one of our most important current foreign policy objectives. It is also one of the most difficult to achieve. In no other field of American public enterprise is the personnel problem more challenging and more urgent. The sheer magnitude and complexity of the program clearly calls for the highest-quality personnel.

When our major post-war foreign aid efforts began, such a body of personnel was brought together. Some of them are still serving with AID. Many of the best, however, have departed. Replenishment with personnel of comparable quality has been increasingly difficult, due in no small measure to the uncertainties and changes mentioned above. The unfavorable reputation of the Agency in the eyes of some American citizens has contributed to this difficulty. But a main source, the Committee is convinced, has been the failure to establish a recognized career service and professional status for persons engaged in foreign assistance work.

Present personnel arrangements are largely the result of improvisation. As early as 1948, it was decided not to incorporate the overseas personnel of the ECA within the regular Foreign Service of the State Department. The general pattern remains about as it was at the beginning. Most professional personnel overseas are employed as Foreign Service Reserve Officers. These are supplemented by Staff and "local" employees. AID employs a total of about 15,500 persons. Its Washington Civil Service includes about 2,500 persons. Its foreign service numbers about 13,000, of whom some 4,300 are United States citizens and the remainder foreign nationals. The overseas staff is dispersed in about 80 countries, almost exclusively in the underdeveloped regions in Asia, Africa, and Latin America. In addition, it utilizes overseas almost 1,600 employees of contractors and more than 500 employees on temporary detail from other Federal departments and agencies.*

Reserve appointments in AID may be made "for the duration of [its] operations," and are not limited to a stated period of time, as they are in USIA and the State Department. This "Reserve" designation, therefore, is a misnomer in terms of its originally intended use as a temporary hiring device. In consequence, a substantial portion of AID's Reserve officers have been with the Agency and its predecessors for many years; a few date their service from 1941 with the Coordina-

*Data as of June 25, 1962.

25

tor of Inter-American Affairs.* Clearly, the Agency has a substantial nucleus of what amount to career personnel even in the absence of a formally constituted career service.

Though AID is legally a part of the State Department, its personnel practices for overseas employees differ markedly from those of the Department. Much greater reliance is placed on direct appointments at all levels of professional work, supplemented by contractual employment. AID hires relatively few junior professionals through competitive nationwide examinations. Its promotion and assignment practices have given more weight to functional specialization than have those of the Foreign Service.

The Committee believes that the conduct of foreign aid programs would be greatly enhanced by the statutory establishment of a career system for core personnel. A career system would make for greater stability and continuity, facilitate recruitment of qualified people, including junior professional candidates, encourage able employees to remain with the organization, and generally contribute to the security, prestige, and morale of the entire staff. It would make possible the institution of improved personnel practices and provide insurance against political patronage. Most of all, it would provide a much-needed recognition of the professional nature of work in the foreign development field and the continuing importance of that work.

Nevertheless, the majority of officer personnel engaged in foreign assistance work abroad should not be included in the career service.** These would include most specialists engaged in specific technical assistance projects in such fields as engineering, public health, agriculture, education, and many others. Many of these specialists expect to resume their careers on the domestic scene. For them, the Reserve designation is entirely appropriate.

But it is not enough to rely on short-term personnel. The program requires a substantial nucleus of career officers, widely experienced in the foreign field and with the problems of development, possessing area and language competence, and willing to serve where needed. Such a cadre would plan, manage, and coordinate the work of the other specialists. The Committee estimates that a career professional foreign service would comprise less than one-quarter of the total number of United States citizen foreign service personnel (including employees of contractors and of other Federal agencies) who are engaged in carrying out foreign assistance programs. In terms of

---

*Nearly half of AID's present foreign service personnel have been with the Agency or its predecessors for five years or more, and more than one-eighth have ten years or more of such service.

**Proposals concerning non-career specialist personnel for overseas development activities are treated in Chapter IX of this report.

current employment, this would mean a cadre of about 1,500 persons. The members of this service would be used in filling positions of mission directors and deputy directors and in providing the core professional staffs of country program offices, administrative, financial, and logistical support sections, and the directing positions in each of the major functional specialties.

In recommending a development career service of limited size, the Committee does not assume the indefinite continuation of foreign aid programs. The requirements for competent people in the rapidly changing field of foreign affairs are such that the members of such a service would represent an asset of great value in other foreign affairs activities should their present responsibilities contract.

The Committee believes that personnel presently engaged in foreign assistance activities should be screened on the basis of a careful evaluation of their qualifications and fitness analogous perhaps to the in-service examination process that USIA used in developing its Career Reserve group. In other words, the Committee does not envisage a blanketing-in process without proper examination of credentials.

Some groups in the past have recommended complete integration of AID personnel with the Department of State. Likewise, there has been increasing effort over the past several years to bring the AID organization into closer working relationship, both at home and abroad, with the organization of the State Department. The Committee found that many AID missions overseas were integrated reasonably well in the total work of the diplomatic establishments under the United States ambassadors, and that others are moving in this direction. The question of whether AID should be organizationally consolidated with the existing structure of the Department of State is outside the scope of the Committee's terms of reference. The Committee's proposal to establish a career professional foreign service would, however, facilitate complete integration, in terms of both personnel and structure, should it be desired in the future. To integrate the personnel systems under existing circumstances would complicate underlying problems of administration and would have the unhappy effect of divorcing personnel authority and responsibility from organizational responsibility.

A FAMILY OF COMPATIBLE FOREIGN AFFAIRS SERVICES

The Committee's recommendations to establish a Foreign Information Service and a Foreign Development Service should be viewed in the light of the following recommendation, which the Committee regards as fundamental.

Recommendation 6

The Foreign Service, the Foreign Information Service, and the Foreign Development Service should constitute a family of compatible services governed by uniform statutory provisions regarding personnel management. In the administration of these services there should be:

(a) substantial uniformity in personnel policies and equality in conditions of service;

(b) joint conduct of personnel operations wherever desirable;

(c) systematic interchange of personnel and provision for lateral transfer; and

(d) consideration of senior personnel of all three services in filling top executive posts in foreign affairs.

Though their missions differ, these three agencies are dedicated to a common over-all objective, a fact which in itself argues for parallel personnel arrangements. Furthermore, each needs personnel committed to serve where needed and adaptable to overseas environments. Each requires flexibility in the assignment of people. Certain training needs are common to all. All three would profit from more interchange of personnel.

The Committee believes that the respective foreign services should be organized as a family of parallel services to be administered within the framework of a basically uniform personnel system. It might later prove desirable to include within this family of services some of the career personnel of other Government agencies, such as the Peace Corps, whose predominant responsibilities are in the foreign affairs field. The question of whether the family of services should encompass overseas personnel of one or more domestic departments with substantial foreign policy interests is discussed in connection with Recommendation 11 below.

The Committee stresses the importance of achieving a substantial degree of comparability in personnel policies, standards, and conditions of service, including appointment, tours of duty, separation, performance evaluation, retirement, and, to the extent international comity permits, overseas benefits and privileges. A number of personnel operations can and should be jointly or centrally administered; these include joint recruitment and examination of junior officer candidates, and central provision for training. The senior career personnel of the three agencies' foreign services should constitute a pool to be drawn on in filling key executive positions both *within* and *across* agency lines, specifically including ambassadorial posts. An expanded program of interagency assignments is urgently needed. If

Foreign Service Officers are to be groomed to fill positions of command and leadership, they should have experience in foreign information and foreign development activities. Program officers in AID and public affairs officers in USIA, as examples, would clearly profit from experience outside their immediate agencies. Such assignments should be prized, not shunned. Finally, provision should be made to permit the lateral transfer of personnel across career service lines, subject to a suitable assessment of their qualifications and need for their services.

All these measures, most of which are discussed more fully in subsequent chapters, should contribute to the development of more productive officers in all three agencies. They should help in breaking down separate and sometimes conflicting points of view. They should make possible more effective utilization of manpower, especially at the crucial executive levels. They should make for more efficient and economical personnel administration.

COORDINATION OF PERSONNEL POLICIES AND PROGRAMS
Recommendation 7

An interagency Board of Foreign Affairs Personnel should be established to assist the proposed Executive Under Secretary of State in bringing about parallel personnel policies and, where desirable, joint personnel operations. Each agency should have primary responsibility for personnel actions affecting individual employees.

The proposed Executive Under Secretary of State should assume leadership in bringing about compatible personnel policies and programs within the family of services. He should be assisted in this task by a full-time professional staff headed by a foreign affairs officer of a rank of at least class 1. He should be further assisted by, and should chair, a Board of Foreign Affairs Personnel to include representatives of the State Department, AID, and USIA of at least Assistant Secretary rank, and a member of the Civil Service Commission. The Secretary of State should be free to add additional members. The Committee has in mind the special interests of the Departments of Commerce and Labor, which are now represented on the Board of the Foreign Service. That board would be replaced by the proposed new Board of Foreign Affairs Personnel. The Committee suggests that the new board be established by executive rather than legislative action.

The Board of Foreign Affairs Personnel should be responsible for recommending common personnel policies and programs. It can play a vital role in making recommendations, for example, on the nature and content of personnel legislation; uniform personnel policies on promotion, tours of duty, and performance evaluation, with due regard to individual agency needs; joint programs of recruitment, examination, and training; a systematic program of interchange of personnel; and suitable programs and standards for inspection. In addition, this board would assess periodically the caliber and qualifications of senior career personnel of the respective agencies and develop lists of those who merit consideration by agency heads in filling key executive and other high-level positions. As a corollary, it would stimulate a program of lateral transfer of able officers across agency lines consistent with manpower needs and interests. It would also work toward removal of inequities and unwarranted disparities in comparative benefits accorded personnel abroad. This task would call for positive efforts to provide overseas personnel with adequate supporting services, especially in such matters as housing, recreation, educational facilities, and medical care and protection.

The Committee regards the proposed board as an indispensable mechanism for achieving compatible personnel systems. Although its functions would necessarily be advisory, the Committee believes that the considered views of the board would be given full weight by each agency. In order that personnel authority may be commensurate with organizational responsibility, however, each agency head should have primary responsibility for personnel actions affecting individual employees.

PERSONNEL IN THE UNITED STATES

The Committee has emphasized the importance of compatible personnel systems for the respective foreign services of the State Department, USIA, and AID. It is also important that the systems which apply to the domestic personnel of the three agencies contribute to the most effective conduct of our foreign affairs.

Recommendation 8

The personnel of the foreign affairs agencies in the United States who are now in the Civil Service system should be redesignated as foreign affairs officers and employees and should be brought within the structure of the foreign affairs services. These employees should not be obligated to serve abroad as a consequence of this redesignation. Future recruitment should, however, stress availability for overseas service, and the long-range goal should be to increase the proportion of personnel available for service at home and abroad. The agendas and the Civil Service Commission should reach appropriate agreements to insure harmonious and mutually beneficial personnel relationships.

The foreign affairs agencies administer their personnel under two entirely different systems. One derives its authority largely from the Foreign Service Act of 1946, as amended, and is used to employ Foreign Service Officer, Reserve, and Staff personnel as well as local nationals. Agency heads have wide discretion in determining personnel policies governing these employees. The Foreign Service system affords great flexibility in the assignment of personnel by virtue of the fact that it identifies salary with the individual regardless of the classification grade of the position occupied. Provisions relating to appointment, compensation, promotion, and many other phases of personnel management are unique to the Foreign Service system.

Most domestic employees—who are not normally required to serve abroad—come under the Civil Service personnel system. The laws governing the Civil Service, and the regulations prescribed thereunder by the Civil Service Commission, are designed for departments and other agencies of the Government generally. The Civil Service system lacks the Foreign Service's flexibility in assignment and transfer of personnel. Every employee's grade and salary is determined by the classification grade of the position he occupies. The rules, policies, and procedures governing virtually every personnel action, from recruitment to retirement, differ from those applicable to Foreign Service Officers.

THE DEPARTMENT OF STATE

The problems of administering two separate personnel systems in the State Department have been complicated as a result of the integration program that grew out of the recommendations of the Wriston Committee in 1954.* The intent of this program was to enlarge the Foreign Service Officer Corps and to provide for the staffing of most professional positions in Washington with Foreign Service Officers. About 630 departmental Civil Service employees were integrated as Foreign Service Officers in the process, although some civil servants who elected not to enter the Foreign Service are still serving the Department. There are today about 2,200 departmental employees at

---

*The Report of the Secretary's Public Committee on Personnel—commonly known under the name of its Chairman, Henry M. Wriston—was published in June 1954 under the title *Toward a Stronger Foreign Service*. This report is best known for its recommendation regarding the integration of Civil Service and Foreign Service personnel.

professional and subprofessional levels—that is, General Schedule grade 7 and above. A commendable purpose of the integration program was to make possible more frequent assignment of Foreign Service Officers to the United States. About 1,250 Foreign Service Officers are so assigned today, in contrast with 200 in 1954. Despite this accomplishment, some unresolved problems can no longer be ignored.

The problems of continuity and specialization. A high degree of specialized knowledge is required in staffing many departmental positions. Civil Service employees tend to remain in a particular specialty for some years and thereby develop background knowledge that is not easily replaced. Rotational assignment of Foreign Service Officers to headquarters positions results in some loss of continuity under the best of circumstances. Unfortunately, too many Foreign Service Officers lack professional interest in departmental assignments in many fields. For example, in a study conducted this year, only 1.2 per cent of Foreign Service Officers indicated primary preference for four functional specialties involving work primarily or exclusively in Washington (public affairs, cultural affairs, international organization affairs, and intelligence and research). Most prefer to remain in the mainstream of the Foreign Service, which they consider affords better promotion opportunities.

At the same time, it is increasingly difficult to attract qualified people through the Civil Service for professional careers in a number of important areas of the Department's work. Professional positions in such fields as economic affairs, intelligence and research, international organization affairs, and public affairs, particularly at the senior levels, are staffed heavily by Foreign Service Officers and Reserve Officers. Departmental officials have testified that they cannot in good conscience offer genuine career opportunities to young college aspirants interested in working in these fields with the Department in Washington: In effect, "If you want a career in State, you had better go into the Foreign Service." The table below indicates the extent to which departmental positions at General Schedule grades 7 and above are filled by Civil Service employees in selected functional activities. It may be noted that the bulk of the positions in administration are filled by civil servants; the Department has not had the same difficulty in staffing administrative posts as it has in the other functional fields referred to above. The replenishment problem is becoming more serious as the number of experienced civil servants who elected not to enter the Foreign Service under the Wriston Program diminishes.

Staffing of State Department Positions in Principal Fields at GS-7 and Above*

Function	No. of Positions	No. Filled by Civil Service	Percentage Filled by Civil Service
Administration	1,811	1,456	80
Consular affairs	105	55	52
Economic affairs	249	77	21
Intelligence and Research	205	116	56
International Organization affairs	93	30	32
Political affairs	372	82	22
Public affairs	294	128	44
Total	3,129	1,944	62

*Public affairs includes cultural and educational affairs. Data as of April 30, 1962.

The problem of replenishment was recently illustrated when a senior State Department official visited a major university to recruit graduate students trained for research work on overseas areas. He was unable to interest a single student in working in a Civil Service position in the Bureau of Research and Intelligence. The reason: promotional opportunities were considered to be too limited.

The inability of the Department to meet its domestic professional staffing needs through the Civil Service, coupled with the relative shortage of Foreign Service Officers qualified in specialized fields, has encouraged the use of the Foreign Service Reserve Corps as a "safety valve" for domestic appointments. The number of Reserve Officers serving in Washington has risen dramatically, from 15 in 1954 to about 400 today.

The problem of equity. While Civil Service officers recognize the need for and desirability of rotational assignment of Foreign Service Officers to departmental positions, their morale and, hence, effectiveness is adversely affected when Foreign Service Officers receive what appears to them to be the lion's share of training assignments, the preferred jobs, and promotions. They resent the fact that Foreign Service Officers frequently receive higher salaries than they do for work of equal responsibility. (The reverse situation, however, also occurs rather frequently.) They find it necessary to "break in" new Foreign Service Officers whose promotional ceilings are not blocked. In contrast, they see their own promotional opportunities restricted. They note with displeasure the continuing influx of Foreign Service Reserve Officers at high levels. All of this is not to suggest that the Department is divided into two hostile camps. It is to point out that the two divergent systems create real and tangible morale problems, particularly in those areas of the Department's work where Civil Service and Foreign Service professional personnel converge.

The problem of inflexibility. In comparison with many of the features of the Foreign Service system, the Civil Service system is quite inflexible. This is most apparent in the linkage of an employee's salary to the classification grade of the position he occupies. This in turn seriously restricts the Secretary's ability to deploy his staff to meet the Department's needs. This inflexibility is compounded by the Veterans Preference Act and regulations prescribed thereunder for administering reductions in force. The Committee was astounded by the tremendous wastage of effort, and the generally inadequate results, in the Department's most recent (1961-62) reduction-in-force program affecting domestic employees.

The problem of dual administration. The necessity of operating a large and complex organization under different laws, regulations, and standards unnecessarily complicates day-to-day personnel management of the State Department. The existence of two dissimilar systems adds obvious strains and stresses which hinder the development of a responsive and forward-looking personnel program. While many of these operating difficulties are not of spectacular moment, their cumulative impact is serious.

USIA AND AID

The staffing profiles of the headquarters offices of USIA and AID contrast sharply with those of the State Department. Neither agency has undertaken to integrate its domestic and overseas staffs. Their headquarters offices are preponderantly under Civil Service—about 90 per cent in both cases as opposed to 68 per cent in the State Department. Neither agency, therefore, is able to assign overseas personnel to Washington to the extent the State Department does.* The Committee believes all three agencies should follow a consistent policy for systematic assignment of career foreign service employees to headquarters. The lack of flexibility imposed by the Civil Service system and the general problem of administering two personnel systems also apply to USIA and AID. Moreover, if the family-of-services concept is to be realized, it follows that USIA and AID should operate within the same basic personnel framework as the State Department.

The Committee believes that many of the difficulties mentioned

---

*The Foreign Service Act requires that Foreign Service Officers spend at least three of their first fifteen years in the Service on assignment to the United States. Current policy is to return officers after six years of overseas service, normally for a four-year Washington assignment.

above would be alleviated by a direct conversion of all the personnel of the foreign affairs agencies from the Civil Service into the foreign affairs services. They would be governed by basic policies, regulations, personnel practices, and standards for the most part comparable to those of the other members of the foreign affairs services. These personnel would differ only to the extent that, in various professional specialties, they would be employed in the future with varying degrees of commitment to accept overseas assignment—in some professional specialties, perhaps frequently or occasionally; in others, perhaps none at all. Civil Service personnel now employed in the agencies should not be required, on conversion, to accept any greater degree of obligation to undertake assignments abroad without their consent than they now have.

Action along those lines would not, of course, solve all the problems cited above; but it should facilitate corrective improvements in many ways. Among these are:

- enlarging the scope and flexibility of the agencies' authority in the assignment and utilization of all their personnel;
- reducing the divisive force of two entirely different personnel categories doing the same work, with its attendant threats to *esprit de corps;*
- encouraging the development of better career possibilities for those in Washington and thus reducing the problem of replenishment;
- reducing, perhaps over the years entirely eliminating, the necessity for dual administration of the various personnel activities, from recruitment through separation, and thus making possible personnel programs that are both more effective and more economical.

The Committee proposes further that in future recruitment and selection, the agencies endeavor, to the extent feasible, to maximize the employment of personnel available for assignment both at home and abroad. Thus, ultimately the great bulk of the positions in Washington would be filled by such personnel.

The proposed changes should be undertaken only after the most careful planning by the agencies themselves. The Committee suggests that in this planning the following principles and objectives be pursued:

1. All foreign affairs personnel should be administered within a unified personnel framework analogous to the Foreign Service system in respect to such basic matters as: rank-in-man; salary; recruitment, selection, assignment, and promotion on the basis of competitive merit within broadly defined lines of career specialization; and selection-out.

2. Under these arrangements the clerical, technical, and subprofessional employees now under the Civil Service would likewise be included within the proposed foreign affairs services.* Over a period of years it should be possible to increase the proportion of clerical employees available for service both at home and abroad. One reason for doing so would be to decrease the costly turnover that now characterizes clerical staffing of overseas posts.

3. Personnel management should be governed solely by the criteria of competitive merit and fitness, and these criteria should be guaranteed by legislative provision and administrative regulations.

4. Present Civil Service employees should be converted to the foreign affairs services at appropriate grades without salary loss. They would be under no greater obligation to serve abroad without their consent than they are at present.

5. The new services should bear a harmonious and mutually helpful relationship to the Civil Service. For example, foreign affairs employees could acquire Civil Service status under an agreement to be negotiated with the Civil Service Commission, as has already been done by employees of some other agencies outside the Civil Service (for example, the Atomic Energy Commission and the Tennessee Valley Authority). The Civil Service Commission should assist the foreign affairs agencies in their recruitment and selection as needed. The agencies should work closely with the Civil Service Commission on personnel problems of joint concern.

6. Employees now under the Civil Service Retirement System should remain under that system pending further study of retirement benefits. Consideration should be given in such a study to providing additional credit toward retirement eligibility for employees who undertake one or more tours of duty abroad. Those who complete an appreciable period of overseas service (for example, five to ten years) could be transferred to the Foreign Service Retirement System.

The Committee emphasizes that its proposals would in no way weaken the merit principle that underlies the Civil Service system, nor would they force present domestic employees to serve abroad. Rather the objective is to bring about more compatible and efficient personnel arrangements for staffing the headquarters organizations of the three agencies and allow for greater flexibility in the future.

---

*Some special groups might be left undisturbed, such as the several hundred State Department employees who work for the International Water and Boundary Commission and are located in Texas.

THE PERSONNEL STRUCTURE

At present, there is much diversity and inconsistency in the provisions that prescribe the various categories of foreign affairs personnel, including provisions governing compensation, authority relative to appointment and promotion, and the commissioning of diplomatic and consular officers. The several categories of Foreign Service personnel include:

1. *Chiefs of Diplomatic Mission* (ambassadors, ministers, and chargés d'affaires): appointed by the President, by and with the advice and consent of the Senate; divided into four classes.
2. *Foreign Service Officers:* appointed by the President, by and with the advice and consent of the Senate and concurrently so appointed and commissioned as diplomatic and consular officers; divided into ten classes, including FSO-8 through FSO-1, career minister, and career ambassador.
3. *Foreign Service Reserve Officers:* appointed by the Secretary of State and, in appropriate instances, appointed and commissioned as diplomatic or consular officers by the President subject to Senate confirmation; divided into eight classes paralleling FSO-8 through FSO-1.
4. *Foreign Service Staff Officers and Employees:* appointed by the Secretary of State and, in appropriate instances, appointed and commissioned as a consul or vice-consul, the latter by action of the Secretary, the former by the President subject to Senate confirmation; divided into ten classes, different from the classes of Foreign Service Officers.
5. *Local Employees or Foreign Nationals:* appointed by the Secretary and compensated in line with prevailing local wages.

USIA and AID utilize only the Reserve, Staff, and local employee categories in their foreign services. Appointment authority rests with the agency head, except that AID mission chiefs and deputy mission chiefs are appointed by the President. Subject to the approval of the Secretary of State, USIA and AID overseas personnel may be commissioned as diplomatic and consular officers. AID relies principally on bilateral agreements with host governments to accord its overseas United States employees many privileges accorded diplomatic officers; relatively few of its personnel are commissioned as diplomatic or consular officers.

As already discussed, all three agencies now employ domestic personnel under the Federal Civil Service system. Appointment authority for these employees rests with the agency head, and their compensation is according to Government-wide pay legislation. Each agency also has authority to appoint experts and consultants.

Recommendation 9

Personnel should be categorized so as to distinguish between career and non-career and between professional and non-professional employees.* The respective services of the State Department, USIA, and AID should be distinctly and separately identified. United States citizen personnel in all categories should be under a single grade structure and salary scale.

In respect to the large body of personnel who are citizens of the United States and who are compensated in accordance with a statutory salary schedule, the Committee believes that the following guides should be observed in distinguishing them:

1. The personnel of the three foreign affairs agencies should be referred to generically as "foreign affairs officers and employees."
2. Personnel of the Department of State should be designated "foreign service officers and employees"; those of USIA, "foreign information officers and employees"; and those of AID, "foreign development officers and employees."
3. A distinction should be made between those who are employed on a career basis and those who are given purely temporary or limited-duration appointments. The generic term "reserve officer or employee" should apply to the latter group.
4. A distinction should be made between professional personnel and clerical, technical, and auxiliary support personnel. The generic term "staff officer or employee," as at present, should apply to the latter group.

The main categories of United States citizen personnel who constitute foreign affairs officers and employees would then be as follows:

Department of State	USIA	AID
Foreign Service Officers	Foreign Information Officers	Foreign Development Officers
Foreign Service Staff Officers and Employees	Foreign Information Staff Officers and Employees	Foreign Development Staff Officers and Employees
Foreign Service Reserve Officers and Employees	Foreign Information Reserve Officers and Employees	Foreign Development Reserve Officers and Employees

---

*In this connection, "professional" is used to distinguish between career and reserve officers, on the one hand, and staff officers and employees, on the other.

Existing statutory salary scales applicable to Foreign Service Officers, Foreign Service Staff, and Civil Service employees are different. These scales should be merged into a single schedule, and tied to the Government-wide salary structure. The officer category in the several foreign affairs agencies would consist of eight numbered classes as at present, supplemented by the classes of career minister and career ambassador.

Recommendation 10

Authority for appointments and promotions in the foreign affairs services should be vested in the agency heads, subject to standards and procedures prescribed by law and regulation, with the following exceptions:*

(a) appointments of professional career officer personnel at class 5 or higher should be made by the President with Senatorial confirmation;

(b) appointments of chiefs of diplomatic missions and of AID mission chiefs whose positions warrant a salary equivalent to that of chief of diplomatic mission should be made by the President with Senatorial confirmation;

(c) promotions to the ranks of career minister and career ambassador should be made by the President with Senatorial confirmation.

Commissions to serve in diplomatic or consular capacities should be granted to the overseas career officers of all three foreign affairs agencies at the time they receive their Presidential appointments. Otherwise, such commissions or equivalent non-commissioned designations should be granted as required on an individual basis, subject to the approval of the Secretary of State.

Career Officer Appointments. At the present time, initial appointments to the Foreign Service Officer Corps are made in every case by the President of the United States, by and with the advice and consent of the Senate. Most of these appointments are to class 8, the bottom level of entry. Officers in the Reserve, Staff, and Civil Service categories are appointed by the agency head; consequently, the pro-

---

*This recommendation is not intended to change existing provisions of law which stipulate appointments by the President, other than those enumerated.

fessional personnel of AID and USIA, with the few exceptions noted below, do not receive Presidential appointments. If the officers of the Foreign Information Service and the Foreign Development Service are to be accorded status and prestige equivalent to that of Foreign Service Officers, they should receive Presidential-confirmation appointments in the same fashion.

The Committee believes that appointments of officers in all three agencies at junior levels (classes 8 through 6) should be made by the respective agency heads. Only on the attainment of class 5, which is here considered to be the basic level of full-scale officer responsibility, should such personnel receive Presidential-confirmation appointments. This proposal is predicated upon concepts developed in subsequent chapters of this report that the lowest three officer classes should be primarily for on-the-job training and familiarization and that promotions through these three classes should normally be rapid. Appointments by the President to class 5 would be made only following a most careful review and evaluation of each officer's performance and potential. Such designation would become a mark of true attainment and distinction. Under these proposals, most officers would attain class 5 when they were between 28 and 33 years old.

The principal reason for this proposal is that the over-all recognition, distinction, and solidarity of the officer groups would be significantly enhanced if the honor of Presidential appointments were reserved for those fully prepared to take on full officer responsibilities. The title "foreign affairs officer" would itself assume greater significance. It may be argued that Foreign Service Officers of class 8 are analogous to second lieutenants and ensigns in the military services, who *are* appointed by the President. The analogy is hardly apt, however, since the junior military officers normally have already had an arduous period of training and indoctrination in one of the service academies or in the reserve officer training program. Initial appointees to the Foreign Service enter on the basis only of examination, with no comparable period of training or evaluation of their performance. In its studies, the Committee has found little, if any, evidence that Presidential appointments constitute a significant incentive for recruitment. In fact, there is some feeling that individuals who would be swayed by this factor may not be the most desirable recruits for foreign affairs work.

Appointments of Overseas Mission Chiefs for AID. At the present time, all chiefs and deputy chiefs of AID missions overseas are appointed by the President, but Senatorial confirmation is not required. There appears to be little logic for this practice, since many of these posts involve lesser responsibilities and considerably lower salaries than do those of other officers who are not designated by the President. Furthermore, there would be a distinct advantage in recognizing these positions as part of the normal career ladder.

Some of the AID mission chiefs of the larger overseas programs, however, have responsibilities, and receive salaries, comparable to those of ambassadors to the smaller and medium-sized countries. The Committee therefore proposes that the AID mission chiefs who are authorized salaries at least equivalent to that of the lowest class of ambassador should be appointed by the President, by and with the advice and consent of the Senate.

Promotions. Under present law, promotions of Foreign Service Officers at every stage from class 8 to career ambassador are made by the President, by and with the advice and consent of the Senate. Promotions of all other personnel, including all personnel of USIA and AID, are made on authority of the head of the agency. This requirement with regard to Foreign Service Officer promotions appears to serve no useful purpose; furthermore, it delays the process of promotion, often for many months, and occasions a great deal of unnecessary procedure and paper work.

On the other hand, the Committee believes that promotions to levels of highest distinction in foreign affairs, career ministers and career ambassadors, and promotions to class 5 (which would be considered as new appointments) should continue to be made by the President with Senatorial confirmation. All other promotions should be made by the agency head.

Commissions. Foreign Service Officers are now appointed and commissioned as diplomatic and consular officers regardless of whether such status is necessary to an officer's specific assignment abroad. The commissioning of USIA officers as diplomatic or consular officers, in contrast, is handled on an individual basis. The Committee believes that persons who are given full professional career officer appointments and are available for service overseas in any of the foreign affairs agencies should be commissioned to serve in a diplomatic or consular capacity.

With regard to junior officers, the Secretary of State can grant the commission, when needed, of vice-consul, as he can today for officers of the Foreign Service Staff; if diplomatic status is indicated, he can, as at present, confer the designation of attaché or assistant attaché. Any other instance in which it is necessary to commission a person as a diplomatic or consular officer should be handled on an individual "as needed" basis, subject to prior approval of the Secretary of State.

ATTACHÉ SERVICES OF DOMESTIC AGENCIES

In addition to the personnel of the Department of Defense, who are not covered in this report, and of the foreign affairs agencies, the United States Government employs a substantial number of professional personnel overseas whose work is primarily for domestic agencies of the Government. Some of these personnel are very clearly in the business of framing, negotiating, and carrying out foreign policy; the work of others, while less directly involved, has important foreign policy implications; still others perform work that is an extension abroad of purely domestic responsibilities.* This last group includes, for example, personnel engaged in the provision of benefits to veterans overseas, the conduct of research programs overseas, and the inspection and quarantine of agricultural products destined for United States markets. Such personnel are normally employed under the Civil Service system and are not treated in this report. Personnel engaged in activities having foreign policy implications, however, deserve special consideration, particularly in their relation to the Foreign Service of the United States and to the State Department.

ATTACHÉ GROUPS WITHIN THE FOREIGN SERVICE

Most overseas activities of interest to domestic agencies are performed by Foreign Service Officers and Foreign Service Reserve Officers. An example is the work performed by labor attachés. Although these attachés are employees of the Department of State, the Department of Labor has an important voice in personnel actions affecting them. In the case of Foreign Service Officers who specialize in international labor matters, the Department of Labor is consulted on their assignments, is represented as an observer on the Foreign Service boards that consider their promotions, and provides needed specialized training. It also nominates qualified persons to the Department of State for temporary assignment abroad as Foreign Service Reserve Officers with international labor functions. Variations on this type of arrangement are civil aviation attachés, who perform work of concern to the Federal Aviation Agency, and minerals attachés who are similarly related to the Department of the Interior.

A further variant is that defined in the agreement of November 15, 1961, between the Departments of State and Commerce, which accords the Department of Commerce a formal voice in decisions

*As of June 30, 1961, twenty domestic agencies employed some 1,700 United States citizens abroad, or about 5 per cent of the total number of such civilian personnel employed in foreign areas by the Government.

concerning the recruitment, examination, selection, assignment, training, and promotion of commercial specialists in the Foreign Service. The agreement provides for formal recognition of commercial specialization as one of the options in the written entrance examination and as one of the functional specialties that Foreign Service Officers may pursue on a career basis. It also provides that the Department of Commerce shall have budgetary responsibility for any expansion of overseas commercial activities conducted by the Foreign Service.

SEPARATE ATTACHÉ SERVICE

An alternative arrangement is found in the separate foreign services maintained by the Departments of Agriculture and the Treasury. Their overseas personnel, though subject to the over-all direction of the United States ambassadors in the countries to which they are assigned, are not members of the Foreign Service of the United States. They receive their instructions from and report to their parent agency in Washington. Treasury and agricultural attachés represent the United States in dealing with foreign governments and hence are accorded diplomatic status. These employees are under the Civil Service personnel system.

The variety of overseas activities of domestic agencies is growing. In addition to those enumerated above, there are other overseas personnel of domestic agencies with foreign policy functions whose relationship to the Department of State and the Foreign Service needs careful consideration. The current overseas activities of the Atomic Energy Commission's scientific representatives, and the proposed overseas education and social welfare activities of the Department of Health, Education, and Welfare, are examples.

Recommendation 11

The Foreign Service of the United States should, as a general rule, serve as the vehicle for those overseas activities of the other agencies of the Government which, though primarily domestic, have an important bearing on foreign policy; for this purpose, its personnel administration should be modified to accommodate better the needs and interests of those agencies. If it should be necessary to make an exception for a large overseas program of such a domestic agency, its overseas personnel should constitute a member of the family of foreign affairs services.

As emphasized in Chapter II of this report, the Department of State has a proper concern in all overseas activities with significant foreign policy implications. It is essential that these activities be carried out within the framework of United States foreign policy objectives and country program plans and that overseas representatives of the various agencies speak with one voice. Other executive departments and agencies of the Government, however, have statutory responsibilities which require overseas representation, and which also have a bearing on the achievement of foreign policy objectives. In short, there is a legitimate duality of interests.

The Committee is convinced that, in the context of the new diplomacy, further proliferation of separate foreign services by domestic agencies would jeopardize the responsibility of the Secretary of State in guiding our foreign policy. It believes that the arrangement best calculated to achieve a desirable balance is one in which overseas personnel engaged in such activities are members of the Foreign Service of the United States, provided, however, that: (1) the personnel management of the Foreign Service is modified to accommodate the specialized overseas interests of the domestic agencies concerned; and (2) these agencies are assured a substantial voice in decisions affecting personnel assigned to perform work in their behalf.

More specifically, the Committee recommends the following guiding principles for the conduct of overseas activities of domestic agencies with a significant relationship to United States foreign policy and its execution:

1. The establishment of new foreign affairs services abroad leading to the further proliferation of personnel systems among the various departments and agencies of the Government should be avoided.

2. With respect to overseas activities now carried out by the Foreign Service of the United States in behalf of other domestic agencies, these agencies should participate in decisions affecting personnel assigned to perform such work, but full budgetary and financial responsibility should be vested in the Department of State. The Committee sees no reason to permit the creation of overseas personnel systems by the departments and agencies now developing new program interests abroad and urges that efforts be made to accommodate them within the Foreign Service of the United States.

3. The Foreign Service personnel system should be so modified with respect to recruitment, examination, selection, training, assignments, and promotions, as recommended elsewhere in this report, as to accommodate the specialized overseas interests of domestic agencies.

4. If the arrangements and modifications referred to above prove successful, consideration should at a later date be given to bringing into the Foreign Service of the United States the overseas

personnel of the Foreign Agricultural Service of the Department of Agriculture and the Treasury representatives or attachés of the Department of the Treasury.

5. Whatever the arrangement, the Secretary of State should have authority to review and approve or disapprove proposed programs, major assignments, and budgets in every overseas country for all such activities, and the ambassadors should continue to direct and supervise these activities insofar as they affect United States representation and policy.

While the Committee believes that the national interest would best be served by the recommendation outlined above, it also recognizes the practical difficulties, especially in the near future, of applying such a recommendation without exception. If it should prove necessary to permit, for the time being, a separate personnel system for any of the larger overseas programs with a substantial bearing on foreign policy, the Committee recommends that such a system be organized as a member of the proposed family of foreign affairs services.

IV

THE KINDS AND

ATTRIBUTES

OF PERSONNEL

*"What we need to know is everything
there is. What we need to know
cannot be accomplished in a man's
lifetime. But we need to delve deeply
into many fields in order that we as
policy makers can make policy with
understanding."*

DEAN RUSK *(in remarks to the
Foreign Service Association)*

SUMMARY

In this chapter are presented the Committee's views concerning
the attributes and qualifications that are especially to be sought
and cultivated among foreign affairs personnel at professional
levels. These are discussed under four categories of need: (a)
general qualities of mind and character, (b) executive ability,
(c) specialized functional competences, and (d) area knowledge.

ONE STRIKING CHARACTERISTIC of the new diplomacy is the diversity
of activities it encompasses and, therefore, the diversity of skills and
knowledge it requires. It is no longer useful to think of foreign affairs
as a single professional field. Rather, it is a broad spectrum into which
a number of professions, some of the orthodox domestic variety and
others peculiar to foreign affairs, must be fitted and modified. Equally
striking is the premium this very diversity places on the capacity to
coordinate activities, to synthesize points of view, and to achieve a
sense of unity and common purpose.

The qualitative requirements for successful performance in foreign affairs may be grouped in four basic categories: (a) general qualities, (b) executive ability, (c) specialized competences, and (d) area knowledge. These four are not mutually exclusive. Each of the agencies must develop specialists in the professional fields pertinent to it, and each must develop executives capable of providing leadership. Some of the best executives are drawn from the ranks of the specialists. Moreover, both specialists and executives should possess the general qualities of mind and character essential to effectiveness in foreign affairs, and both must be equipped with deep understanding of foreign environments. Each of the four basic requirements is discussed briefly below.

GENERAL QUALITIES

Discussion of general qualities needed in foreign affairs is clouded by the semantic confusion attending the term "generalist," which has long been associated with Foreign Service Officers. In one sense, "generalist" refers to a man's ability to do a variety of things or to perform satisfactorily any task within the limited universe of tasks for which a particular organization exercises responsibility. Before World War II, this concept could be applied more realistically to the Foreign Service than is true today. Its relevance is now essentially confined to positions in small diplomatic and consular posts.

At times "generalist" is used in referring to an officer engaged in political reporting, analysis, and negotiations. This is, however, misleading, since political officers are often as specialized—and their responsibilities are as specialized—as others in our embassies. In fact, virtually all officers abroad, whether labeled political or not, need a broad understanding of political factors as well as social and economic ones.

In another sense, "generalist" refers to a person with ability to comprehend the ends and means with which an organization is involved and the relation of his own role to the totality of organizational activity. This kind of comprehension is devoutly to be desired in *all* foreign affairs employees, especially those at professional levels.

In a fourth sense, the term is equated with "executive." This practice tends to rob both words of utility. It assumes that the hallmarks of an executive are his ability to perform well a variety of activities and his understanding of the total picture. But useful and necessary as these general qualities may be, they are not the same thing as leadership and managerial ability.

It is important to be clear about the need for seeking out and developing persons who are not only expert in a particular phase or aspect of foreign affairs work, but also possess a breadth of understanding of the objectives and instruments of foreign policy. The professional man in foreign affairs cannot be concerned only with his own field of competence. He must understand and appreciate the role of the other professional fields; he must relate the specific to the general, the part to the whole. Additionally, he should, if he is to assume major responsibilities, develop the happy faculty of grasping essentials and applying his knowledge and skills effectively within and across a range of disciplines. This is the sense in which the Committee considers the term "generalist" useful today.

Any listing of desirable qualities risks committing the "paragon fallacy" of setting up standards that no one person could possibly fulfill. Nevertheless, four qualities appear to the Committee vital in the foreign affairs field. Every effort should be made to seek out, and to develop, persons who possess these qualities:

1. *Zeal for creative accomplishment.* Traditional diplomacy has emphasized observing, reporting, and quiet negotiation. These activities still play an important role in our foreign affairs. At the same time, the new diplomacy relies heavily on operating programs, the techniques of which are still being evolved. The strong program orientations of the United States Information Agency and the Agency for International Development tend to attract persons concerned with the more visible evidences of action; this turn of mind is also becoming more apparent among the Department of State's Foreign Service Officers. The Committee here emphasizes that United States foreign policy today calls for substantial numbers of persons strongly disposed to creative accomplishment and action.

2. *Deep understanding of life and culture at home.* Before he can operate effectively in a foreign environment, the officer overseas must know his own. Recruitment programs should place special emphasis on knowledge of the American heritage and institutions, a knowledge that must be continually refreshed. One of the salutary effects of the Wriston Program is that it facilitated the systematic re-exposure of Foreign Service Officers to the domestic scene. The need for such re-exposure remains a critical problem for AID and USIA. The former agency displays a peculiar imbalance. On the one hand, many of the persons who have been with the foreign assistance program for a substantial number of years run the risk of becoming virtually expatriated. On

the other hand, AID uses a great many short-term specialists who, while they may have deep roots in American society, do not stay overseas long enough to develop any deep familiarity with the foreign society. The danger of cultural expatriation is especially grave in USIA because it is this agency's special responsibility to transmit appreciation of our life and culture.

3. *Ability to communicate effectively across cultural barriers* and to develop a sympathetic understanding of other peoples and their cultural heritages. The art of *cross*-cultural communication requires insight into the foreign environment coupled with retention at all times of one's own national identity. Possession of this quality is made more imperative by the geographic expansion of United States foreign affairs representation abroad, encompassing as it now does most of the less familiar cultures of the world.

4. *Adaptability and flexibility.* The capacity to adjust one's self and one's work to new environments and associations, altered directions in policy, and changing work demands and techniques is particularly crucial in a career foreign service where, of necessity, officers must be prepared to serve at a variety of posts and must expect occasional assignments outside their area of preference or specialization. The importance of this requirement was driven home during the Committee's visits to thirty-two posts abroad. Many of the officers interviewed had experienced rapid shifts in the place and nature of their assignments as well as almost day-to-day shifts in the demands placed upon them in their individual jobs. Clearly, professional foreign affairs work has no place for the rigid or routinized mind or for the person who is unable to adapt to change, however well developed his technical competence may be.

EXECUTIVE ABILITY

The professional fields within foreign affairs are not ends in themselves; they must be subordinated to the demands of policy, and they must be coordinated to the goals of program accomplishment. Leadership in welding specialized capacities to produce decisions and carry out policy objectives calls for a high level of executive talent, above and beyond specialized ability.

The number of positions of command and leadership in foreign affairs at home and abroad is astonishingly high. For example, there are now over one hundred United States diplomatic missions overseas, almost all of which require an ambassador, and most of which include a deputy chief of mission with a comparable scope of responsibility. Some of these are of such size and importance that the key supporting positions in the fields of political, economic, consular, and administrative affairs also qualify as truly executive. There are many consular offices of considerable size and importance outside the capital cities; indeed, some of these are more demanding of executive talents than some of the embassies. AID is conducting programs in approximately eighty countries, and most of these call for a chief and deputy chief of the AID mission; the larger missions require additional administrators with a high order of executive ability. In most countries abroad, the role of the public affairs officers and some deputy public affairs officers in USIA missions requires a high level of executive talent.

The demands are no less striking at home. There are in the State Department approximately two hundred positions in the line of command at the level of deputy office director or higher. Additional officers at comparable levels in AID and USIA would double this figure. All told, about 1,000 positions at the present time in these three agencies, at home and abroad, may properly be considered "executive." This number has been going up rapidly ever since World War II. There is every reason to believe it will continue to rise as new countries emerge, as new international instrumentalities are created, and as new functional fields of concern to the United States develop.

The proportion of top executive positions to the total number of officers who might aspire to those positions is unusually high in foreign affairs. This should be seen as an advantage and an inducement to the officers within the several services and to prospective officers in the future. Few fields of professional activity and few, if any, organizations can offer greater opportunity and greater challenge to their officer personnel than the foreign affairs programs and their agencies.

The requirements for effective leadership in foreign affairs today are unusually demanding and difficult to satisfy. The normal attributes of executive ability in domestic organizations are not the only needs. The executive in foreign affairs must also have: a broad understanding of historical forces and of the interplay of intangibles in the body politic, both at home and abroad; an awareness and sensitivity to the possibilities of, and the means and effects of, social change; and an ability to grasp and utilize the full range of political, economic, military, social, psychological, and scientific instruments in the international field. These requirements cannot be met through experience only in the traditional mold of the diplomat: a striking illustration of the new dimensions of diplomacy is the extent to which economic problems have come to occupy the time of virtually all ambassadors abroad as well as many executives at home. In addition, top executives must comprehend the mechanics of government administration, and be able to use the specialized techniques and procedures of management without letting them become ends in themselves. In using the terms "executive" and "administrative" in this report, the Committee means precisely this combination of an appreciation of higher policy considerations and an ability to use the practical tools of management—the combination required by the new nature of diplomacy.

Many of these qualifications are not readily produced in the normal streams of American experience, and must be developed largely within the organizations themselves. The maintenance of a nucleus of qualified foreign affairs executives demands a career system. But it is clear to the Committee that the traditional career system for Foreign Service Officers in the Department of State is inadequate, and in some respects wrongly directed, to develop some of the qualities needed. The favored route to the top in the Foreign Service has been political work; yet most activity within this field is singularly devoid of supervisory or managerial responsibilities.

In this connection, it is interesting to note that present leadership in the State Department, both at home and overseas, includes only a minority of officers who entered and progressed in the Foreign Service by the orthodox examination route. The table below makes this clear. In the Department in Washington, fewer than one-fifth of the executive positions, deputy office director and above, are now held by examination officers.* About 36 per cent are held by officers who entered laterally,** and the remainder are filled by Reserve Officers, civil servants, and political appointees. Overseas, some 32 chiefs of mission are examination officers, less than a third of the total and barely more than the 30 who entered laterally. All posts of deputy chief of mission are filled by Foreign Service Officers, but the majority of these, almost two-thirds, are held by lateral entry officers.

---

* The term "examination officers" is used herein to describe those Foreign Service Officers who entered the Service originally by examination at the lowest officer level. They also include three who entered as a result of the Rogers Act of 1924.

**These include persons who entered the Service under a variety of mid-career entry programs back to 1939, the largest of which by far was the Wriston Program in the mid-1950's.

CATEGORIES AND MODES OF ENTRY OF EXECUTIVES IN STATE DEPARTMENT, 1962

Categories and Modes of Entry	Department Deputy Office Directors and above [a] (Oct. 1962)		Field Chiefs of Mission (July 1962)		Deputy Chiefs of Mission (July 1962)		Total	
	No.	%	No.	%	No.	%	No.	%
Foreign Service Officers								
Examination Entry	40	18.8	32	31.7	36	37.5	108	26.4
Lateral: Pre-Wriston	23	10.8	23	22.8	39	40.6	85	20.7
Lateral: Wriston and later	53	24.9	7	6.9	21	21.9	81	19.8
Foreign Service Reserve Officers [b]	26	12.2	—	—	—	—	26	6.3
Civil Service and Political	71	33.3	39	38.6	—	—	110	26.8
TOTAL	213	100.0	101	100.0	96	100.0	410	100.0

a. Includes only positions in the line of command.
b. Includes one Foreign Service Staff Officer and three officers on detail from other agencies (two from AID, one from USIA).

Foreign development work is particularly demanding of executive talent. AID programs entail heavy operational responsibilities, and most of them operate exclusively in the areas of the world where the forces of change are moving most rapidly. There is almost no way to obtain experience in the United States in coordinating the special interests of a variety of technical fields and fitting them into the complex, changing needs of total societies. The need for sustained development programs for executives in foreign assistance work is critical.

International information work appears to be a good field in which to develop a broad view, a sensitivity to other cultures, an action frame of mind, and program experience. But, as presently set up, USIA has a more limited opportunity to utilize executive talent than do the other agencies. Moreover, the program of USIA is by nature relatively specialized. Consequently, if its best executives are to qualify themselves for broader leadership posts in foreign affairs, they need at some point to acquire experience outside the Agency itself.

SPECIALIZED COMPETENCES

The variety of professional skills required for the conduct of foreign affairs is in direct proportion to the greatly increased scope, complexity, and magnitude of the United States' role in foreign affairs. Unless the need for specialized competences is fully recognized, especially in initial selection of personnel and in their subsequent assignment, promotion, development, and training, our successes may be more than matched by our failures. It is particularly important that the foreign affairs agencies draw on the best professional resources of the United States and that professional skills not readily obtainable on the outside be nurtured and strengthened by imaginative in-service programs of training and development.

DEPARTMENT OF STATE

The problem of specialization has been acute in the Foreign Service of the State Department for many years. The need for providing efficient and flexible means of acquiring specialists in all fields was recognized in the Foreign Service Act of 1946. Heavy reliance, however, was placed on the Foreign Service Reserve and Foreign Service Staff categories to provide specialists and technicians. The Foreign Service Officer Corps itself was conceived more as a "generalist" arm, the members of which would enter for the most part at the bottom and, if not selected-out, would advance by merit to fill positions of command and leadership.

Every major personnel study of the Foreign Service since the enactment of the Foreign Service Act has called for increased recognition of specialization in the Foreign Service Officer category. The Wriston Committee, in its report of 1954, laid particular emphasis on the need for specialists. Its proposals for enlarging the Foreign Service Officer Corps by the integration of Civil Service, Foreign Service Reserve, and Foreign Service Staff personnel were designed in part to strengthen the specialized capabilities of the career Foreign Service. Other recommendations relating to recruitment, training, career development, and promotion were also aimed at this objective.

In practice, however, the Wriston integration program itself did not materially augment the total personnel resources available to the Secretary of State either in terms of specialists or generalists. Rather, it converted into Foreign Service Officers a large number of employees then in the departmental service and in the Foreign Service Reserve and Staff branches.

As pointed out in Chapter III, the Department is finding it difficult to attract career-minded specialists to fill some Civil Service positions in Washington. It is also finding it difficult to maintain continuity and develop sustained professional interest among Foreign Service Officers in many of the more specialized phases of the Department's activities. Junior Foreign Service Officers are still largely recruited from the academic disciplines traditionally associated with the Foreign Service—history, international relations, and political science—and there has been a conspicuous short-fall in the fields in which specialization is most needed, such as economics and administration. The proportion of Foreign Service Officer appointments

54

at mid-career levels, a potential source of seasoned specialists, has been declining over the past three years. The promotion system for Foreign Service Officers is commonly regarded as not affording equal prospects for specialists. The substantial increase in the use made of the Foreign Service Reserve is further evidence that the State Department is not meeting its needs for specialized talents through the Foreign Service Officer Corps. In short, the Department does not now have enough qualified people in its career professional Foreign Service in a number of fields, and little replenishment is coming up through the ranks. Fortunately, this condition now appears to be receiving the more thoughtful attention it deserves.

Thus, in retrospect, the Department of State has not yet modified its personnel policies and operations to the extent necessary to achieve the objectives advocated by the Wriston Committee with respect to specialization. While the Department's effectuation of the integration program undoubtedly strengthened the specialized capabilities of the career Foreign Service, at least temporarily, the net effect has been to weaken the depth and continuity of specialized competences in Washington. Furthermore, the nature of the personnel system has encouraged many of those integrated into the Foreign Service Officer Corps to flee from their specializations. There are acute shortages of persons who combine specialized knowledge in the fields listed below with experience and broad understanding of foreign affairs. In all these fields, the needs can be expected to grow in the future:

a. Economists with practical competence in planning economic and social development, including specialists in international trade and other fields.
b. Other social scientists, particularly those equipped to deal with problems of social and political development in the newer nations.
c. Management specialists.
d. Politico-military experts.
e. Persons experienced in international organization affairs.
f. Experts in all aspects of obtaining and analyzing intelligence.

UNITED STATES INFORMATION AGENCY

USIA does not appear to have significant shortages of persons skilled in the various communications media. There are ample reservoirs of talent to draw on in the United States. The real problem is to find persons skilled in the arts and techniques of persuasion who also know their own society well and are capable of operating effectively in foreign environments. Hence, the needs for "Americanization" and for area and language specialization bear particularly heavily upon USIA.

Moreover, USIA's growing program responsibilities in Asia, Africa, and Latin America are creating needs for new kinds of communications practitioners abroad. In many cases, USIA may have less need for specialists with extensive experience in communications media than for young and energetic persons who can adapt the media to new situations and the unusual conditions prevailing in remote regions. Many of USIA's junior officers appear well suited to this kind of activity. The growing importance of the less-developed regions of the world in USIA's program plans may call for increased informational contributions to modernization programs. Growth in these directions obviously heightens USIA's need for stepped-up emphasis on area specialization and for expanded training programs. It calls for more social-science analysts with knowledge of communications theory and techniques, and for new programs of research into the communications aspects of social and political change.

AGENCY FOR INTERNATIONAL DEVELOPMENT

The creation of AID in 1961 was premised upon several concepts that may heavily influence the nature of specialized personnel needs in foreign assistance work. These concepts include: emphasis, in AID's own efforts, on planning and advising other governments, on request, rather than actually operating development projects overseas; maximum encouragement of host-country planning and operating; substantial delegation of authority to regional offices and, through them, to field missions; maintenance of a relatively small permanent core of programers and specialists; and increasing reliance on the specialized resources of other institutions through means other than direct hire.

How far and how effectively AID will move in these directions remains a matter of conjecture. The numbers and kinds of personnel it will need can be estimated only after the Agency has clarified the policies it will pursue in these regards. There is no question, however, that qualified specialists will be needed in a considerable variety of fields for some time to come. The majority of these will probably be temporary employees, either hired directly by the Agency or obtained through contract arrangements with other employers. There will also unquestionably be a continuing need for a relatively small career core of specialists, qualified in these same functional fields, but capable also of planning, directing, advising, and supervising development activities. In Chapter III, the Committee has proposed that this nucleus of development specialists be incorporated into the proposed Foreign Development Service. An illustrative list of specialists, divided between those who might properly be regarded as temporary and those who would constitute the career group, is shown below.*

AID FOREIGN SERVICE SPECIALISTS AS OF FEBRUARY 1962

Personnel Category	Total	Career	Temporary
Agriculture	745	50	695
Industry and Mining	234	34	200
Transportation	96	11	85
Labor	38	9	29
Health and Sanitation	220	16	204
Education	356	52	304
Public Administration	108	43	65
Public Safety	131	26	105
Community Development	47	15	32
Housing	38	16	22
Private Enterprise	13	—	13
Participant Training	87	87	—
Communications Media	86	28	58
Procurement and Supply	65	65	—
Washington Complement	123	—	123[a]
General and Miscellaneous	90	1	89
Total	2,477	453	2,024

a. Includes an unknown number of employees who are "career."

The concern of this chapter is only for the career group of specialists.** It appears essential that this group, comprising the planners, negotiators, advisers, and supervisors of AID programs both at home and abroad, include persons well qualified in their technical fields who are also experienced in, and have an understanding of: the AID program; the objectives and workings of the United States Government; and, particularly, foreign policy and overseas activities.

There is a growing need for recognition of the professional quality of development work and for conscious stimulation of the development aspects of existing professions. Development economics is already established, but such recognition is only beginning in other important development fields such as administration, public health, education, and communications. The establishment of a career service

*This division is based on a study made in February 1962, in which the distinction between career and temporary was made after an analysis of positions then occupied. The table does not include about 1,700 contract employees utilized on AID projects, over 500 employees of other Federal agencies employed overseas on AID projects, and almost 100 overseas consultants.

**Chapter IX deals with non-career specialists for overseas development.

as recommended in Chapter III would itself contribute to the professional character of development work. A number of proposals in subsequent chapters of this report should likewise contribute to it.

AREA KNOWLEDGE

The importance of foreign affairs for the United States, and the necessarily strong orientation of our foreign policy in the direction of program accomplishment, requires an understanding of the forces of change in foreign societies of a depth never before contemplated. Area specialization is not itself a profession, except perhaps in the academic world. The foreign environment is the factor peculiar to foreign affairs which requires the modifying and synthesizing of the professions. Area knowledge is a requisite in each professional field of foreign affairs. For those serving overseas, area knowledge frequently needs to be coupled with foreign language competence.

While all three agencies require a high degree of flexibility in the deployment of their personnel, each agency must develop expanded programs of area specialization for virtually all functional fields. This is necessary for the improvement of cross-cultural skills.

The Committee does not have in mind the classic image of the scholar steeped in the culture and history of a region. It is more important that an officer be steeped in the problems of United States foreign policy in a given area and at the same time be able to communicate effectively with people in different strata of foreign societies. He should be better attuned to the changes of today and the past thirty years—particularly in the rapidly evolving regions of Africa, Asia, and Latin America—and he should think in terms of ongoing responsibility for the management of United States interests in the country and region of his specialization.

Area specialization is not new in the Department of State. The European and Latin American "circuits" and the "old China hands" existed well before World War II. More recently, Arabists and Soviet and Eastern European specialists have been developed. The number of Japanese and other Far Eastern and South Asian specialists has grown, and the drive to staff the new African posts is creating specialists in that area. Increasing interest in area specialization stems largely from the feeling of many Foreign Service Officers that a good way to reach the top, in a larger and more diversified service, is to become a "double specialist"—that is, both a specialist in political work and an area specialist.

There is little in the way of articulated policy regarding area specialization, no discernible system for gauging the need for area specialists or for relating area to functional specialization. A consciously designed program stressing continuity, improvement of cross-cultural understanding on the part of all officers, and a sense of individual responsibility for the course of events in various areas and countries is needed.

The same shortcomings are found in USIA and AID, and these agencies are unable to offer even the informal inducements that encourage many Foreign Service Officers to take up area specialization. These agencies may need area specialization even more than the State Department because their programs require them to communicate across cultural barriers to whole populations and to key segments of populations.

Familiarity with an area needs to be supplemented by proficiency in foreign languages. The Department of State (and to a lesser extent USIA) has made significant progress in raising the level and extending the scope of the language competence of its Foreign Service Officers; the Committee believes that the career foreign service personnel of USIA and AID should seek to match the standard of the Department of State.

A DESIGN FOR STRENGTHENING THE PROFESSIONAL SERVICES

"The basic test of the effectiveness of an organization is a functional one: how well it helps to marshal the available human and material resources to do the job for which it was created."

THE BROOKINGS INSTITUTION, 1960

SUMMARY

In this chapter are presented underlying objectives of the Committee for the management of the three professional career services. More specific proposals are contained in subsequent chapters. Central, and also preliminary, to all of these recommendations is the establishment of machinery whereby future manpower needs may be anticipated and used to guide other personnel activities.

EACH MEMBER OF THE FAMILY OF SERVICES should have as its nucleus a career corps of professional personnel serving both at home and abroad. A significant proportion of recruits in each corps would come in at or near the bottom of the career ladder and develop their talents through a variety of planned assignments and training; some would ultimately qualify for the highest positions in foreign affairs. The Committee believes that personnel practices in all three agencies must be changed in a number of respects to make them better suited to meet the demands of the new diplomacy. The principal objectives of these changes are to provide:

1. a system whereby estimates of present and future personnel needs of the foreign affairs agencies will guide all personnel activities;
2. a basis for better interagency coordination, greater understanding by the services of each other's programs and problems, and a greater sense of unity of purpose;
3. methods whereby the rich professional personnel resources of the United States can be tapped for foreign affairs by (1) more positive recruitment efforts; (2) appointment as junior officers of persons in their twenties or early thirties who have already proven themselves in higher education and professional experience; and (3) a program of career appointments above the junior officer level to the extent needed to provide an invigorating flow of fresh blood and, especially, to meet agency requirements for specialized skills;
4. a reduction in the time interval between original appointment and advancement of junior officers to full officer-level responsibilities through planned and supervised internship and rapid promotion of those who meet a high standard of performance;
5. positive incentives and adequate machinery for assuring that personnel in the several services acquire specialization in the areas and disciplines needed by the foreign affairs agencies;
6. an expanded system of post-entry training to meet the general as well as the particular needs of the foreign affairs agencies, and a high-level government educational institution to provide and to guide professional training in foreign affairs work;
7. procedures whereby officers will undergo an especially thorough review of their qualifications and potential before advancement to the mid-career level, and again before advancement to the senior level; and
8. procedures whereby executive and leadership talents of experienced officers can be identified, developed, and better utilized by the foreign affairs agencies within and across agency lines.

The Committee envisages the three closely related foreign affairs services as being responsive to the needs of the nation and at the same time offering challenging and satisfying careers to all their members. They would be managed with a conscious effort to develop qualified leadership for the international problems of tomorrow. They would be built on a base of new recruits who on the average would be somewhat older and more experienced than has been true in the Foreign Service in the past, but not to the exclusion of a positive program for seeking out outstanding talent at all levels. Those recruited at the junior levels who meet a high standard would progress more rapidly to full professional responsibilities, and over the years the average ages of officers at intermediate and senior levels would decline. In these services, functional lines of professional work would be clearly and equally recognized in the basic personnel processes—recruitment, selection, assignment, promotion, and training—although specialization should not be pursued to the detriment of qualities demanded of all professional personnel in foreign affairs work. All foreign affairs officers should have the general qualities described in Chapter IV, and the discovery and cultivation of such qualities in the services should be an important consideration in the recruitment and selection of new officers and in the training and assignment of those already employed.

PLANNING OF FUTURE NEEDS

A *sine qua non* for carrying out all the specific proposals that follow in this report is a system for estimating, as far in the future and as specifically as possible, the numbers and kinds of people who will be needed by the foreign affairs agencies. In its own explorations, the Committee found that it could not accurately assess personnel needs in any of the three agencies; machinery is lacking whereby program objectives are spelled out in terms of the personnel resources required to accomplish them.

Recommendation 12

Manpower planning machinery should be established in each agency to assess manpower requirements in the light of program plans and other pertinent information and to project such requirements, with periodic review and adjustment, five to ten years in advance in terms of numbers, kinds, and deployment of personnel.

A large part of the personnel effort today is devoted to "fire-fighting." As things now stand, little consistent preparation can be made for meeting probable future requirements and little insurance can be provided against unforeseeable contingencies. Acute personnel shortages in some areas exist alongside of surpluses in others. In the State Department this situation has been due in part to difficulties in programing the use of available funds. Money initially appropriated for personnel transfers and travel, for example, has been diverted to other purposes to meet unforeseen and emergency needs. Consequently, the Department has repeatedly had to defer travel and home leaves. Under these circumstances, consistent personnel planning has been well-nigh impossible.

Advance estimation of personnel requirements in the field of foreign affairs is uniquely important and also uniquely difficult. The importance derives from the importance of foreign affairs work itself, and the tremendous dependence in this work upon the qualitative excellence of the human beings who make the decisions and who carry them out.

The extraordinary difficulty is due in part to the sheer uncertainties that confront the foreign affairs agencies as well as to the global scope of United States interests and commitments. Furthermore, the qualities and skills needed in filling many foreign affairs positions are not readily available in the manpower market place. They must be developed from within the services through a series of experiences and tailored programs of training. Indeed, this purposeful internal improvement of talent is a main justification for a career service. One of the penalties of a career service, however, is that lead-time between initial selection and readiness to assume full responsibilities at the executive level is unusually long. This means in turn that personnel needs must be projected some years in advance in order to provide an informed basis for personnel planning, with particular reference to recruitment, career development, and training programs. The difficulty of the task should not be an excuse for neglecting it.

Manpower planning is an element of the programing discussed in Chapter II, and it should be carried on under the general guidance of the Executive Under Secretary. Units for this purpose should be set up under the chief administrative officer in each agency. These units should:

1. regularly study new and projected programs and policies and interpret them in terms of the numbers and kinds of personnel they will require;
2. work with the operating bureaus in the estimation of future manpower needs and in the development of the personnel aspects of budgets;
3. integrate these estimates into total agency-wide estimates of manpower needs by number and type;
4. develop and recommend goals, criteria, and guidelines with respect to recruitment, career development, training, and assignment of personnel; and
5. coordinate their work and findings with those of the other foreign affairs agencies.

For these purposes, the units should systematically search for and analyze information concerning present and probable future programs and their personnel implications, both in qualitative and quantitative terms. These studies should, of course, encompass the full range of foreign affairs activities of their agencies, both abroad and at home,

VI

NEW PEOPLE

FOR FOREIGN

AFFAIRS

"The overriding requirement for an effective foreign policy is a rapid broadening of its personnel base. The wider the base the more talent the Department of State and the Foreign Service will eventually be able to draw upon for reinforcing their senior personnel at the highest levels of diplomacy."

THE WRISTON COMMITTEE

SUMMARY

In order to ensure a continuing intake of personnel to meet the diverse and demanding requirements of the new diplomacy:

- in the recruitment, examination, and selection of junior officers for foreign affairs careers:

    (a) a greater effort should be made to attract young persons with graduate education and professional work experience; in consequence the entering level for junior professional appointments should include class 6 as well as 7 and 8;

    (b) AID should regularly recruit a substantial proportion of junior officers;

    (c) recruiting machinery of the three foreign affairs agencies should be merged, recruitment sources extended, and recruitment methods strengthened; and

    (d) the examination processes should be consolidated, speeded up, and improved. Special effort should be made to bring into the career services of the three agencies persons with needed specialized preparation through such measures as provision in the written examination for a series of options in different subject-matter fields;

- recruitment of junior officers should be supplemented by a program to seek out and bring into the career services at intermediate and higher levels experienced persons of high quality, particularly to meet specialized needs, subject to thorough examination; and
- a positive recruitment program and competitive examining process should be used in the appointment of Reserve Officers for limited periods of service.

AS NOTED IN CHAPTER III, the foreign affairs agencies operate under two distinctly different personnel systems. Most of the departmental or headquarters positions in all three agencies are filled by persons recruited under the Civil Service system. Foreign service personnel are recruited under the Foreign Service system, which is applied differently in each of the three agencies. The Department of State, for example, relies heavily (as it has for many years) on the recruitment of young college graduates who are brought in as junior Foreign Service Officers. In recent years, junior officer appointments have accounted for about four-fifths of the total number of Foreign Service Officer appointments.

The Agency for International Development has relied almost exclusively on recruitment of more mature persons with specialized training and experience brought in at the middle and higher grades.

The United States Information Agency falls in between. While it brings in proportionately more new appointees at intermediate and higher levels than does the Department of State, it also has a positive junior professional recruitment program very similar to that of the State Department.

The Committee wishes to emphasize three key points in regard to recruitment and selection of career professional people for foreign affairs. First, if the over-all quality of the career services is to be improved, the foreign affairs agencies must be able to interest and consistently to attract dynamic, high-caliber junior people. Second, the agencies must be able to select the best of those who apply in terms of their future personnel needs. This requires the perfection of techniques for assessing, in fair and open competition, desirable qualifications and personal qualities. Finally, each agency must strike a balance between recruiting, at the bottom levels, persons of high academic attainment but lacking advanced preparation and work experience, and recruiting more mature, experienced persons at intermediate and higher levels. It is doubtful whether any career service can meet the demands of the new diplomacy if it stakes its replenishment on only one of these alternatives.

The Committee's recommendations in this chapter are designed to meet these three points.

JUNIOR OFFICER RECRUITMENT AND SELECTION
Recommendation 13

The entrance levels of junior officers into the career professional services of the foreign affairs agencies should be classes 8, 7, and 6, the higher of these levels being used to attract more mature persons with advanced education and relevant experience. AID should recruit proportionately more junior officers in staffing its program.

The Department of State and USIA are engaged in separate but similar efforts to recruit junior officer candidates from among top-quality students in colleges and universities throughout the country. In 1961, for example, about 3,800 persons took the State Department's written examination for the Foreign Service and about 1,100 competed in USIA's. The Foreign Service applicants came from over 600 educational institutions and USIA's from over 300.

Junior officer appointments by the Department of State to the Foreign Service are primarily to class 8, though authority exists for appointment to class 7.* USIA has, until very recently, restricted its junior appointments to class 8. The majority of applicants for both agencies have no schooling beyond the bachelor's degree when they compete in the examinations, and very few have earned graduate degrees.** The educational training of these applicants is heavily concentrated in political science or history relative to other disciplines now required in our foreign affairs work.

Recruitment programs and appointment systems directed principally toward college seniors are certain to miss many potential candidates who now go on for graduate work. It is now normal for college graduates of high academic standing to proceed for one or more years of graduate work. A study of 34,000 graduating seniors in 1961 showed that more than 90 per cent of the men and more than three-quarters of the women ranking in the top fifth of their classes expected to go to graduate school.

Entry at Foreign Service class 8, moreover, is not competitive with progressive private firms, or even with the Federal Civil Service, for prospective candidates with much background beyond college. The Civil Service's recruitment program for Management Interns—

---

*Public Law 86-723, approved September 8, 1960, authorized direct appointment to class 7. Among the candidates who were successful in the 1961 oral examination, about one out of six was considered eligible for appointment at this level.

** Seventy-two per cent of the FSO candidates and 66 per cent of the USIA candidates in 1961 had no graduate work. Only 5 per cent of the FSO and 8 per cent of USIA candidates had graduate degrees.

in many ways a sibling of the Foreign Service Officer examination—offers appointments to a level equivalent to FSO class 7 for those with successful graduate work. Others are appointed at a level equivalent to class 8. It is significant that about two-thirds of the Civil Service recruits come in at the higher level.

Finally, the Committee would stress the need in all the foreign affairs agencies for officers with a zeal for creative accomplishment. Individuals with some work experience following completion of their formal education will have had opportunities to develop and demonstrate this quality.

The Committee believes that junior officer recruitment programs should continue to attract, for class 8 entry, highly qualified individuals who want to begin their careers after completing undergraduate training or who, for financial or other reasons, cannot continue their schooling. But the Committee is convinced that the present junior officer recruitment programs of the foreign affairs agencies should be revised to permit them to attract persons with a higher degree of professional interest and attainment, particularly in the functional specialties they require. One important means of accomplishing this is to extend the entering level for junior professional appointment to include class 6, as well as classes 7 and 8. By permitting entry as high as class 6, it should be possible to attract junior professional personnel with graduate education and work experience in many of the specialized fields sorely needed in the foreign affairs agencies. Restricting initial appointment to class 8, or even class 7, unnecessarily deprives the agencies of the flexibility needed to seek out these kinds of persons.

The class at which a junior officer is initially appointed—class 8, 7, or 6—should be determined in each case by his level of maturity as reflected in his education and experience in relation to agency personnel needs. The guiding principle should be that the more education and experience the candidate has had, the higher the class of his initial appointment—with due regard, of course, to a candidate's relative performance in the formal written and oral examinations and other evidences of leadership and growth potential. It might be expected that class 8 appointees would normally be 22 to 24 years old; those appointed at class 7 would be typically 25 to 27; and successful candidates entering at class 6 would usually be in the age range of 28 to 31.

The Committee believes that this broadening of the range of entrance appointment levels, coupled with vigorous recruitment efforts, will contribute greatly to improving the over-all quality of career foreign affairs personnel and will help the agencies acquire the variety of professional expertise necessitated by the new diplomacy.

As noted earlier, AID recruits relatively few junior officers for its foreign service. By and large, AID and its predecessor agencies have depended on finding persons already qualified for performance at middle and senior levels; such persons have generally been drawn from among those who applied on their own initiative or those who could be induced to leave their present employment, inside or outside Government, to take foreign assignments. The Committee believes that the junior officer recruitment programs outlined in this chapter should be used to provide a steady intake of young talent into the professional career service for the conduct of foreign assistance programs, as outlined in Chapter III.

Recommendation 14

The efforts of the Department of State, USIA, and AID to recruit junior officers into their career foreign services should be merged; and their programs should tap more systematically the most promising sources of highly qualified candidates.

At present, the foreign affairs agencies carry out separate and, to some extent, competing recruitment efforts. The State Department and USIA conduct college-relations programs and send representatives throughout the country to talk with students and faculty members regarding employment opportunities. The Committee believes that existing efforts are deficient in the following respects:

1. The quality and caliber of agency recruitment representatives is uneven. Often recruiters lack persuasiveness, and at times actually hurt the cause they are endeavoring to serve.
2. Recruitment efforts are overly concentrated on graduating college seniors; too little attempt is made to reach graduate students and those who have completed their education and are already engaged in law, business, and other professions.
3. Recruitment representatives typically see or speak to only a fraction of the faculty and students, more often than not from comparatively few fields of major study. Whereas students whose major subjects are history, political science, and international relations are well represented in the applicant group, existing efforts have yet to attract enough applicants from the specialties in which critical shortages now exist, such as administration, economics, and the behavioral and natural sciences. For example, over the past several years only 6 to 8 per cent of each year's examination applicants for the Foreign Service have been trained

in economics. A much smaller proportion have had educational background in the other shortage fields.

4. The agencies need to develop more effective relationships with career advisers in universities and colleges. The Committee found that in many instances these advisers are not encouraging their ablest students to seek careers in foreign affairs work. Sometimes this pattern of advice can be traced to the stereotypes such advisers have of the Foreign Service. Some feel that young people with "activist" tendencies will find the Foreign Service frustrating and lacking in opportunity for creative use of their talents. In other instances, career advisers feel that young people from other than white, Protestant, upper-middle-class origins, no matter how able, do not have a good chance of being appointed to the Service, or to advance if appointed, and counsel them against applying.

A strengthened recruitment effort will be all the more vital in order to attract substantial numbers of older applicants at classes 7 and 6.

First and foremost, the several agencies should merge their recruitment programs. Joint recruitment offices ably staffed by trained recruiters should be located at strategic points throughout the country. Recruitment representatives can thereby establish continuing and more effective relations with career advisers in universities and with other potential sources in order to stimulate interest among the persons best qualified to seek foreign affairs careers in any of the foreign affairs agencies.

Second, there should be a much greater effort to reach additional sources of supply. These efforts should be directed at professional and business organizations, other Federal agencies, state and local governmental agencies, and other groups. Well-qualified persons regardless of ethnic or social class origin should be encouraged to apply for junior-level entry in the foreign affairs career services.

There are a number of sources of personnel within the Government itself. First, there are the Foreign Service Staff employees of the three agencies, many of whom are potential officer material. Nor should Civil Service employees throughout the Government be overlooked.

The Peace Corps seems to have captured the imagination of many people who are motivated to serve their country abroad. Volunteers undergo rigorous scrutiny both in a written examination and by observation during training by skilled observers. Very few have failed to adapt to their overseas environments. Many such persons, upon completing foreign tours of duty, may be excellent material for career appointments in one of the foreign affairs career services.

In addition to area knowledge and language skill, some of the volunteers possess pertinent functional skills.

Military personnel who have successfully served in extended overseas assignments are likewise an important potential source of recruitment for the career foreign affairs services.

The Committee has considered various proposals to establish a Government-operated Foreign Service academy which would provide a two- to four-year course of pre-entry education, largely at the undergraduate level, for young people deciding to make a career in foreign affairs. It is the judgment of the Committee that the talent needed can best be produced through our highly decentralized system of education, with its diversity of discipline and richness of experience. The Committee believes further that a coordinated, positive recruitment effort by the three foreign affairs agencies can successfully attract the best products of our educational system.

Recommendation 15

The entrance examining processes of the Department of State, USIA, and AID for junior officers should be strengthened and administered under standards and precepts recommended by a joint Board of Examiners. The importance of relevant specialized education and experience should be recognized through provision of special optional sections in the written examinations.

At present, the Department of State and USIA employ a common written examination which is given on the same day in September at centers throughout the country. Candidates must elect the agency of their choice in advance; they may not apply for both. The sections on general ability, English expression, and foreign languages are similar for all candidates. The general background portion differs as between USIA and State Department candidates. The State Department introduced special options for the first time in the 1962 examination: one including items in executive management and business, and one including items in government and public administration.

It is both feasible and desirable to develop a single written examination, with appropriate options, which can be given to junior officer candidates of all three agencies. A joint Board of Examiners for the three agencies, therefore, should be established, to replace the present Board of Examiners for the Foreign Service. This new board should include representatives of the three foreign affairs agencies and the Civil Service Commission. The joint board should be responsible for developing standards and precepts to govern the examinations for career appointments in the family of foreign affairs services, including written, oral, and other examinations at all levels of entry.

The written examination (as at present) should include a common core of tests that all candidates would take regardless of agency and regardless of major field of study or experience. Provision should be made, however, for a series of options that will take into account the differing needs of the three agencies. For example, in addition to the options recently included in the 1962 examination for the Foreign Service, specialized options might be offered in such fields as economics and economic development, behavioral sciences, American civilization, area specialization, agriculture, and labor. Recognition of the need for competence in given subject fields will help attract well-qualified applicants who now perceive little or no opportunity to use and develop their talents in a foreign affairs career.

Under this arrangement, applicants could opt for the agency of their choice and for the specialty or specialties most appropriate to their talents and interests. To the extent that the same option applies to more than one agency, a common register could be established from which each agency could select successful candidates for appointment.

Measures of traits and abilities that are highly important in foreign affairs work should be included in the examinations. For instance, writing ability is a crucial skill. Recently, the Board of Examiners for the Foreign Service included an evaluation of the candidates' ability to write effectively as an adjunct to the work of the oral examination panels. The Committee suggests that a more systematic examination is needed, and that a professional testing organization develop and grade a suitable standardized test of writing ability. This test would be graded only for those candidates who pass the short-answer portion of the written examination.

The Committee believes that competence in a foreign language should continue to be included in the examination process. Candidates who demonstrate proficiency in one or more foreign languages, or who obtain a satisfactory score on a test of foreign language aptitude, might properly be given additional credit in the final ranking of successful candidates on appointment registers. The Committee does not recommend, however, that a candidate be required to pass a foreign language examination in order to be appointed. This competence, where lacking, can and should be developed by intensive language study after entry but before an officer is advanced to the next higher class.

The current written examinations for junior State Department and USIA foreign service officers are prepared by a professional test-development organization. Unfortunately, this organization does not have sufficient opportunity to assess the predictive ability of the tests it develops. Examination materials should be systematically validated against some measure of job performance.

The oral examining process should be improved. Although examining panels are given common examining precepts, they in fact develop their own criteria. The Committee's studies of oral examining panels show that while each panel tends to be self-consistent, there is considerable variation among panels. Oral panels, moreover, should not attempt to evaluate abilities better examined by written tests. Instead, they should attempt to assess personality traits and skills that cannot be measured through the written examinations.

Both of the foregoing difficulties can be overcome in part by standardizing and refining the techniques of oral examining. Further improvement can be registered by selecting panel members with care and by giving them thorough training in examination processes. Examiners should include outstanding officers in the various major specializations as well as prominent people from Government and private life. By drawing on the resources of all three foreign affairs agencies, it should be possible to obtain the numbers and caliber of personnel required to do this most important job.

The results of the written and oral examination should be collated with all other pertinent information obtained by the joint Board of Examiners in establishing a register or registers from which appointments would be made. The over-all evaluation of test scores, performance in the oral examination, reference letters, and related information concerning character and suitability should be made by professionally trained staff attached to the Board of Examiners.

Recommendation 16

The examination and appointment process for junior officers should be geared to the rhythm of the employment market at academic institutions and should be greatly speeded up.

The competition for promising college graduates and graduate students is increasingly keen among the many potential employers— government, business, professional concerns, and the universities themselves. Many of these have no obligation, as does the Federal Government, to provide competitive examination procedures and to make an exhaustive security investigation. It is becoming standard procedure for such employers to offer appointments, often on a conditional basis, to seniors and graduate students following a single interview. Such offers are frequently made—and accepted—during the winter, many months before the close of the academic year.

The foreign affairs agencies (State Department and USIA, at the present time) are at some intrinsic disadvantage in this race to employ the best products of the universities. Their interviewers cannot offer jobs on the spot, even conditionally. The process of qualifying for a foreign affairs job is necessarily arduous for the applicant. But clearly this competitive disadvantage could be greatly reduced.

During the current academic year, the written examination for the Foreign Service was given in September. The first oral examinations will not begin until January, four months later, and the last will not be completed until June. Job offers will not begin to be made until April, at the earliest; the majority will be made in June, or about the end of the academic year. Meanwhile, of course, a substantial portion of the interested and qualified candidates, including some of the most desirable, will have accepted offers from other employers.

There is no way of measuring how many potentially successful officers, who might otherwise wish to compete, decline to apply for foreign affairs entrance examinations simply because of the long delays and uncertainties which they know to attend the examining and appointment process. But it is clear that, among those who do apply, there is a substantial attrition between application and possible appointment, and that this attrition is particularly marked among the applicants who appear to be best qualified. Many applicants fail to appear for the written test. Among those who pass this test, the loss by withdrawal prior to the oral examination is considerable —about one in four. These dropouts include a high proportion of persons who scored well on the written examination. Of those who pass the oral examinations, a substantial number decline appointments—recently about one-fifth.

One obvious corrective to this situation is to reduce the time required for the process of selection, and a drastic reduction appears to be entirely feasible. Currently, a principal delay results from the slowness in scheduling oral examinations after the written examinations are completed and scored—now nearly four months. It should be possible, through assigning and training examiners in advance and through accelerated scheduling, to reduce this time to about four weeks. A second major delay results from the security-clearance procedure. In fact, only a very small proportion of the otherwise successful candidates are found unsuitable as a result of the clearance procedure, and appointments could be made conditional upon security clearance in any case. If appointments were made following a quick screening for the presence or absence of adverse information, pending full security clearance, great reductions in time would accrue. Appointment offers could thus be made earlier in the academic year, effective on completion of the candidate's academic work.

In addition to speeding the examination process, the foreign affairs agencies might use a variety of other devices to make their employment process more competitive with other employers. Consideration should be given to offering the examination twice or even three times a year rather than only once. Continuous registers might be established on the basis of recurrent competitive qualifying examinations. Separate examinations might be offered for those beyond the undergraduate level. If the recruitment and examining systems of the foreign affairs agencies were merged, as suggested earlier in this chapter, such devices would be more feasible and economical than under the present divided systems.

RECRUITMENT AND SELECTION AT HIGHER LEVELS
Recommendation 17

Recruitment of junior officers should be supplemented by a positive program to seek out and bring into the career services at intermediate and higher levels experienced persons of high quality, particularly to meet specialized needs, subject to rigorous competitive examination.

The Committee considers it essential that the three foreign affairs agencies develop systematic programs for the recruitment, thorough examination, and competitive selection of experienced persons at intermediate and higher levels, particularly to meet specialized needs that are not satisfied through appointments at the bottom levels.

Such action is needed to equip the career services with needed special skills where these cannot be produced adequately through the junior officer recruitment pipeline, or in the agencies themselves, or where fast-changing requirements do not permit enough lead-time for training bottom-level entry officers. A career service also requires the invigoration that comes from a continuing intake of able, mature persons who bring with them differences in outlook, and professional training and experience. Under a suitably rigorous program, outstanding persons from universities, other Government agencies, labor organizations, private business, and other institutions could be attracted to employment in the foreign affairs agencies.

Present policies of the foreign affairs agencies differ greatly. AID relies almost exclusively on direct recruitment at higher levels. USIA also recruits a substantial proportion of its career officers above the junior officer level.

75

In the case of the State Department, the question of lateral appointment to the career Foreign Service has long been a subject of controversy. The Foreign Service Act of 1946 authorized direct appointment of persons with prior Government service as Foreign Service Officers above the bottom of the career ladder, but the framers of the Act clearly envisaged limited use of this authority in order not to jeopardize the career principle.

During World War II, the size of the Foreign Service Officer group actually declined. In order to rebuild the Service to meet its expanding post-war responsibilities and to bring in specialists, authority was obtained in the Manpower Act of 1946 to appoint up to 250 persons as Foreign Service Officers at grades through class 1 over a period of two years. One hundred sixty-six appointments were made under this authority following an aggressive recruitment program and perhaps the most careful and systematic process of screening ever employed for lateral entry into the Foreign Service Officer Corps. It is widely considered that many of the most competent senior officers of the Service today came in under the Manpower Act; in fact, of the original 166 appointees, no fewer than 15 are now ambassadors and 22 are deputy chiefs of mission.

Leaving aside this temporary resort to direct appointment above the bottom entry level, the lateral appointment provisions of the Foreign Service Act of 1946 were used very sparingly until the Wriston Program of integration was launched in 1954. Only 51 such lateral appointments were made from 1946 to 1954—this despite a partial effort, begun in 1951, to amalgamate the departmental service and the Foreign Service.

Reference has already been made in this report to the Wriston Program, whereby the Foreign Service Officer Corps was greatly expanded between 1954 and 1957 by the transfer of departmental Civil Service Officers, Reserve Officers, and Staff personnel to the career Foreign Service. In all, some 1,670 persons were integrated in the process.

Since completion of the Wriston Program, lateral appointments have continued, but on a relatively conservative basis. From 1959 through 1961, a total of about 115 such appointments were made. These appointments, largely concentrated in Foreign Service classes 4 and 3, were drawn almost exclusively from among persons already employed in the State Department under Reserve or Civil Service categories. More significantly, lateral appointments have declined steadily relative to junior officer entry and to Foreign Service Reserve appointments. Whereas in 1959 lateral entrants accounted for about 20 per cent of the total number of Officer and Reserve appointments, in 1961 they fell to slightly under 10 per cent. In relation to all professional recruitment during this period, the relative decline in lateral career appointments is shown below:

Professional Appointments in the Department of State by Category:
Calendar Years 1959-61

	1959		1960		1961	
	No.	%	No.	%	No.	%
FSO Junior Entry	88[a]	40.	166	46.	207	41.
FSO Lateral Entry	35	16.	42	12.	38	7.
FSR	48[a]	22.	92	25.	147[b]	29.
Civil Service (GS-9 and above)	47	22.	63	17.	114[c]	23.
Totals	218	100.	363	100.	506	100.

[a] Projection from number hired between July 1, 1959 and December 31, 1959.
[b] Excludes 8 ambassadorial appointments made pending Senate confirmation.
[c] Excludes 12 Presidential appointments made with Senate confirmation.

The fact of the matter is that the Foreign Service Reserve category is now the *primary* vehicle for obtaining needed skills at intermediate and higher professional levels in the State Department. Whereas Reserve Officer appointments in 1959 constituted 28 per cent of the total number of appointments of Foreign Service and Reserve Officers, they made up about 38 per cent in 1961. More than two-thirds of the Reserve appointments were to fill positions that Foreign Service Officers would normally be expected to staff, including administration, economic affairs, political work, public affairs, consular operations, program direction, international organization affairs, and research and intelligence. It is significant that Reserve Officers do not have to undergo the same competitive examination process as junior Foreign Service Officer candidates.

To remedy this over-all situation, each agency through its manpower planning program should make at least an annual determination of the extent and nature of its requirements for career officers at each level up to class 1. Particular weight should be given to shortages in the more specialized functions and occupations, although due attention should also be paid to needs for higher-level executives. The Committee judges that the majority of such appointments would be at classes 5, 4, and 3, with comparatively few at classes 2 and 1. The total number of lateral appointments to be made in relation to junior officer intake at classes 8, 7, and 6 will undoubtedly vary between agencies and from year to year within each agency. In the case of the State Department, the Committee considers that lateral appointments should normally range up to not more than 25 per cent of the total number of career officer appointments in a given year. This percentage would undoubtedly be too low for AID and might be inadequate to meet USIA's needs.

The Committee believes that mid-career entry should be based on vigorous efforts to seek out and attract, on a highly selective basis, demonstrably superior candidates who are willing to have their qualifications assessed with those of others in fair and open competition. It is not enough to wait for prospective candidates to apply, or for an interested official to encourage someone to make application. Nor should the source of supply be limited to persons already employed in other branches of the agency. Rather, each agency should systematically tap all potential sources, including universities, other Federal agencies, state and local governments, private business, labor organizations, and so forth.

In this connection, the Committee urges that all three agencies make a strenuous effort to attract and make effective use of the talents of outstanding professionally trained women for work at home and abroad. The emergence of women leaders and the expansion of women's groups and activities, especially in the less-developed countries, has focused attention on the growing participation of women in public service. Candidates for appointment at junior levels should be given full and fair consideration regardless of sex; the Committee believes, however, that women are more likely to pursue a *bona fide* career in foreign affairs if they have already manifested professional career interests over a period of years in other lines of endeavor.

The Committee suggests that the three agencies coordinate their middle-entry recruitment efforts to the extent practicable in order to avoid needless duplication. It should be possible to merge recruitment machinery for a number of occupations in the same manner as recommended for junior officer recruitment. The personnel officers of each agency, moreover, should work closely with operating officials, who are more likely to have first-hand knowledge of potential sources of supply in some of the professions pertinent to foreign affairs.

Great harm would be done to the career principle if mid-career entry standards are less than exacting. No person should be appointed to the career services at intermediate and higher levels unless he clearly demonstrates high qualifications in his field or fields of competence. In contrast to the essentially non-competitive examinations used today, the examining process should be competitive. In addition to a searching analysis of all available information concerning the candidate and his previous experience, training, and performance, provision should be made for a thorough oral examination designed to evaluate personality traits and general qualities and to ascertain the candidate's command of his field or fields. The Committee suggests that consideration be given, in some cases, to the development of appropriate written tests, the review of other evidence indicating the candidate's ability to apply his knowledge to problem-solving situations, and his ability to write effectively.

The Committee believes that it should be made possible for the agency heads to make lateral appointments from among outstanding persons who have not previously served the Government. In those instances where a successful candidate has not had the benefit of overseas experience and is being recruited for foreign service, it would seem appropriate that he first serve an overseas tour as a Reserve Officer; but his performance as a Reserve Officer should be equated with that of career officers in the same class and career line for purposes of promotion.

Recommendation 18

A positive recruitment program and vigorous competitive examining process should be used by the foreign affairs agencies in the appointment of Reserve Officers for limited periods of service. The Reserve vehicle should be regarded as a supplement to the career services in meeting temporary and specialized requirements.

The foreign affairs agencies will continue to need well-qualified persons recruited for limited periods of service in various professional capacities, both at home and abroad. The rapidly changing demands of the new diplomacy require that the agencies not rely solely on their career services. The substantial increase in recent years in the number of Reserve Officer appointments in the State Department indicates that neither the Civil Service nor the Foreign Service Officer career cadres have been able to satisfy fully the Department's personnel needs. While the improvements suggested in this report relative to the career services should enable the State Department to fill most of its needs by career people, the Reserve vehicle affords the Department and other agencies a flexible instrument to supplement their career personnel. This is perhaps most apparent in the reliance that AID must continue to place on recruitment of short-term specialists in overseas development activities. The provisions relating to the Foreign Service Reserve Officer category in the Department of State are generally well suited to meet this requirement in all three agencies. The Committee suggests that Reserve appointments be used:

1. to help staff programs or activities of a temporary character;
2. to fill positions of unique specialization where the talent needed can best be obtained by temporary assignment of persons from the outside;
3. to facilitate the temporary assignment in one of the foreign affairs services of persons employed by other Government agencies, such as the Departments of Commerce and Labor, in order to bring about mutually beneficial interchange of personnel; and

4. to bring in, on a probationary basis, well-qualified specialists in fields not adequately staffed by the career services prior to consideration of their possible entry into one of the career services.

The State Department and USIA utilize a screening process to select Reserve Officers that normally includes a panel assessment of candidates' qualifications and fitness. Not infrequently, however, the area of competition is limited to one or very few candidates. The very flexibility and simplicity of Reserve Officer appointments offer a potential threat to the maintenance of the merit principle in the staffing of the foreign affairs agencies. Consequently, the Committee urges that more positive recruitment efforts be undertaken to seek out well-qualified persons for Reserve appointments. Operating officials and personnel recruitment staffs should work together in developing and canvassing promising sources of supply within and outside the public service. This, in turn, should result in greater emphasis on competitive selection. Along with this positive recruitment effort, the agencies should assure that a high standard is maintained in the examining process. In addition to careful scrutiny of qualifications, candidates should undergo an oral examination that will not only probe their proficiency in their particular field of specialization, but also stress those more general qualities and insights which are important in foreign affairs activities. Consideration might also be given to the use of a written examination or other written evidence of problem-solving and writing abilities in appropriate instances. It should be borne in mind that the Reserve provides a potential source of candidates interested in making a career in one of the foreign affairs agencies. In such cases, initial recruitment and examining processes should take into account the possibility of future lateral entry from the Reserve to the career services.

POLICIES AND

TOOLS FOR

PERSONNEL

MANAGEMENT

"What we should aim at producing is men who possess both culture and expert knowledge in some special direction. Their expert knowledge will give them the ground to start from, and their culture will lead them as deep as philosophy and as high as art. We have to remember that the valuable intellectual development is self-development . . ."

ALFRED NORTH WHITEHEAD

SUMMARY

In order to guide the development and utilization of career personnel to meet the requirements of the new diplomacy:

- each foreign affairs agency should establish strong career development programs, to operate within guidelines provided by the manpower planning operations;
- the work of career development should be further ordered by three primary policy orientations: the concept of functional career lines; increased emphasis on area specialization; and differential treatment at each of the three basic career stages —junior, mid-career, and senior;
- the pivotal points of the career stages should be selection into full officer status upon promotion to class 5 and selection into senior status upon promotion to class 2;
- the procedures of promotion panels should be modified to make them more responsive to agency needs for specialized talents and to assure consideration of both specialized competence and general qualifications;
- the ranks of career minister and career ambassador should be open to qualified senior career officers in AID and USIA; the senior executive personnel of the foreign affairs agencies

81

should constitute a pool of talent for key assignment, where appropriate, across agency lines;

- the foreign affairs agencies should each have selection-out authority, but such actions on the basis of time in class should be eliminated;
- appropriate foreign service employees of USIA and AID should be placed under the Foreign Service Retirement System; greater use should be made of present administrative discretion to extend the mandatory retirement age;
- differences in benefits accorded overseas employees of comparable rank and responsibility should be eliminated to the maximum practicable extent.

THE BASIC TASKS of personnel management in any large, complex organization are to provide the human resources needed for current work and at the same time to develop the skills and talents that will be required in the future. Both must be performed with due regard to the interests, desires, and personal problems of the individual employees concerned. These are formidable tasks in any setting. The best people are always in short supply and hence in current demand. Harried executives who must deal with today's problems are not inclined to think in terms of career plans designed to meet needs five to ten years hence.

In foreign affairs, the difficulties are compounded by the sheer complexity and dynamism of our foreign relations, by the tremendous geographic scatter of the field establishments, and by the built-in differences in personnel systems within and among the agencies involved. In addition, the general tendency to splinter personnel management into semi-independent functions is here particularly marked. For example, each agency has separate units or boards for recruitment, examining, promotion, assignment, and training; each has its own point of view and precepts, and tends to go its separate way. These problems make especially urgent the development of policies and tools that will give a unified sense of direction to all aspects of personnel management.

When a choice must be made between urgent present and future needs, it is entirely proper to give priority to the first. And yet a real test of management is the giving of attention to both. This is a test that cannot be met by the personnel office alone. There can be no unified philosophy of personnel management, no adequate attention to the needs of tomorrow, without the full understanding and support of top management and of supervisors down the line.

The proposals that follow are intended to contribute to a consistent philosophy of personnel management—a philosophy that will help weld its parts into a unified whole, accommodate the need for specialized and executive talents, and provide a better basis for striking a balance between present and future personnel needs. These proposals are addressed not alone to personnel officers but to all executives and supervisors.

CAREER DEVELOPMENT

Recommendation 19

The complexity of modern foreign affairs requires that comprehensive career development programs be utilized as a necessary tool of management and that career development units in the three agencies be strengthened.

An effective career development program can be a vital force in bringing unity and cohesion into the complexities of personnel management. It can provide the essential link between manpower needs, present and future, and the talents and interests of individual employees. By its nature, the career development function must be performed with the whole complex of personnel activity in view; in this sense it stands apart from the special interests and pressures of any one operational division of personnel. Thus, the career development unit can serve as a common source of objective information and guidance for all personnel units. By the continued study of the availability of skills in relation to manpower and job-qualification requirements, by the systematic counseling of employees and the preparation of individual career plans, the units engaged in career development will be able to help gauge training needs, point up skill shortages in relation to recruitment planning, provide evaluative material and projections pertinent to promotions, and, above all, provide guidance for the assignments of individual personnel. They should also study requirements of different kinds of jobs at home and abroad, and collate and summarize performance evaluation material.

All three agencies presently have career development organizations, but their functions vary widely. In the Agency for International Development, career development is another name for training. The United States Information Agency has a modest program restricted largely to junior officers. The Department of State initiated its program in 1956 and since then has developed, quite possibly, the most advanced conceptual approach of any civilian agency of the Federal Government. Unfortunately, the impact on operational decisions has been disappointing. The unit in the Department's Office of Personnel responsible for the function has not had adequate manpower planning information on which to base its career planning recommendations. Its staff has been too small and uneven in quality; it has been a repeated target for budget cuts. The career development program was created for the purpose of synchronizing the development of specialists and executives with the demand for them, in the spirit of the Wriston Report, but adequate corresponding changes were not made in the key areas of recruitment and promotion; hence, career development has not been able to exert as significant an influence as it should have.

The career development programs of AID and USIA should be reorganized and modeled on the approach of the State Department's program. In all three agencies, the career development units should be provided with manpower projections, qualified personnel, budgetary support, and well-defined responsibilities. For the staffs of career development units, greater stress should be placed on highly qualified professionals in the field of personnel. The complexity of the programs will require long-term commitment in a full professional sense.

LINES OF SPECIALIZATION
Recommendation 20

The personnel systems and practices of AID, USIA, and the Department of State should be built around a series of flexible career lines representing all major professional fields, including executive direction. Provision should be made for geographic specialization in a number of professional fields and for the development of executives. The highly competent functional specialist should be able to advance to class 1 in his professional field.

In Chapter IV, the Committee identified as of basic importance the needs for: a suitable career climate for the main professional fields in foreign affairs; the development of executive talent; and increased area specialization. In varying degrees, all three agencies have recognized these needs, and yet serious problems remain.

In order to meet the requirements of the new diplomacy for specialists and executives, the Committee believes that the three agencies must assure that adequate recognition is given to the need for expertise and career opportunities in the relevant professional fields. The career-lines proposal, in association with other recommendations in this report, is intended to provide a conceptual basis to which recruitment, assignment, training, and promotion policies can be related. Every officer should be identified with a primary career line, and most officers should have experience in at least two. Examples of functional career lines in the foreign affairs agencies might be:

administrative, economic, political, consular, and public affairs; international organization affairs; cultural affairs; research and intelligence; public health; agriculture; radio; press and publications. The person who is competent in his major functional field, who is needed in that field and would like to stay in it, should not feel compelled to abandon the field in order to get promoted. On the other hand, most officers, especially those likely to attain top executive posts, should have some experience in other fields.

Obviously, the career-lines concept will work only if the individual officer in each specialized field knows that he has every reasonable prospect of reaching class 1 if his competence in his field grows steadily. There is a widely held opinion in all the agencies that some fields of specialization have a low "ceiling," that officers who aspire to class 1 must leave their fields for more favored ones. If long-term commitment and high competence are to be encouraged in these fields, and if new persons are to be attracted to them, then the way to the top grades must be cleared.

In addition to the functional lines, there should be an executive career line for persons occupying or qualified to occupy high executive posts. It would differ from the others in that it would draw its membership from all of them and would constitute a career line only at the higher grades. Recognition of the distinctive character of the major professional fields in foreign affairs should favor, rather than militate against, the development of executive talent. There is ample evidence that extensive experience in one or more subject-matter fields can provide sound preparation for executive responsibility.

Appropriate numbers of persons in most major functional fields should be given training and experience necessary to develop geographic area expertise. The goals of area specialization are to develop knowledge in depth of particular regions and countries and to provide a basis for continuity of assignment and a sense of individual responsibility for the course of events in areas of specialization. These goals apply to virtually all functional fields.

CAREER STAGES
Recommendation 21

The following stages of a foreign affairs career should be explicitly recognized:

(1) junior officers—classes 8, 7, and 6;

(2) mid-career officers—classes 5, 4, and 3;

(3) senior officers—class 2 and higher.

Each of these stages should be distinctively treated from a personnel standpoint.

The Committee believes that there are three discernible stages in a foreign affairs officer's career, each having distinctive characteristics and purposes. Clear recognition of these would make possible personnel policies tailored to the needs and potential of each stage. The junior officers (classes 8, 7, and 6) are essentially in the familiarizing and preparatory stage; the mid-career officers (classes 5, 4, and 3) are engaged in full-scale professional work; the senior officers (classes 2, 1, career minister, and career ambassador) are at the command or expert level. Stages comparable to these may be found in many other organizations, including private businesses and academic institutions, whether or not they are formally acknowledged. The stages here proposed for foreign affairs officers also have certain rough equivalents in the civilian and military services of the Federal Government in terms of role, responsibility, and remuneration. The junior stage compares with junior professionals of the Civil Service at General Schedule grades 7 through 11 and with Army company-grade officers—Second and First Lieutenants and Captains. The mid-career stage approximates the full-scale professionals of the Civil Service, at grades GS-12 through GS-15, and the field-grade officers of the Army—Major, Lieutenant-Colonel, and Colonel. The senior stage is roughly equivalent to the supergrades of the Civil Service, GS-16 through GS-18, and with officers of star rank in the military— Brigadier Generals and above.*

The *junior officer stage* should be basically one of orientation and on-the-job training—an internship in foreign affairs. An officer should spend a minimum of two years in junior status, but advancement of those who meet a high standard should be rapid, the time in grade ranging from nine to twenty-four months at each level. Thus, successful officers would normally reach class 5 between the ages of 28 and 33, on the average about five years younger than is currently true in the Foreign Service. The long-run effect of such a policy would be to lower the average age of officers at middle and senior levels and to make the class structure and salaries of the foreign affairs services more nearly competitive with business and other Government employment.

In organizational terms, the junior officer program in each agency should be planned and controlled by a unit or an affiliate of the

---

*Exact equivalents are impossible to establish among the different personnel systems, but the rough parallels are clear. In some Federal agencies, the grade of GS-11 is considered the top of the junior category; in others, the bottom of the intermediate. Likewise, GS-15 is often considered the bottom level of the senior stage rather than the top of the intermediate. The parallelism with the ranks of assistant, associate, and full professor, which are almost universally recognized in academic institutions, is also worthy of note.

career development program in the central personnel office. Following a short initial course of training in foreign affairs and agency orientation, the time spent by junior officers would be devoted essentially to on-the-job training. All junior officers should have rotational assignments that include service at home and abroad, including at least one brief exposure to the work of another foreign affairs agency. In rotating to different functional fields for short-term experience, junior officers should receive careful supervision, instruction, and evaluation by their superior officers. Both in Washington and in the field, junior officers should participate periodically in seminars with their fellows.

The fact that junior officers, during their tenure in classes 8, 7, and 6, will spend most of their time in job-rotation assignments will have the effect of opening up opportunities for advancement of Foreign Service Staff personnel to assignments at higher grade levels than most can now aspire to. This is in line with the recent Department of State policy announcement aimed at improving the promotional opportunities for the Staff Corps.

On entering the *mid-career stage,* the officer would assume full professional status. Classes 5, 4, and 3 would constitute the operating levels of foreign affairs work, in which the officer would function primarily in his main field of specialization, normally acquire a secondary field, and receive opportunities for demonstrating his capacity to assume executive responsibilities. Interagency experience is particularly important at the mid-career levels. Each officer should have an opportunity to serve a tour of duty with a second foreign affairs agency. The mid-career stage should be introduced by an intensive basic officer training course, to be followed by further periods of more specialized education and training for each individual along the lines of his career development plan. In some cases, this will involve language and area training of some depth. The most capable officers, those who continue to demonstrate capacity for enlarged responsibilities, would normally expect to spend three to five years in each class. It is important to note, however, that some officers will reach their peak at one or another of the mid-career grades. If performing competently, they should be able to remain in grade indefinitely without fear of selection-out.

The *senior stage* of class 2 and above should be regarded as the expert and command level. Only officers who have evidenced a capacity for executive leadership or who have outstanding competence in a professional field should be advanced to the senior stage. The Committee has emphasized the need for top executive talent and for demonstrably superior professional men who will compare favorably with the best men in their fields outside the services. The senior grades should be reserved for persons of this caliber. Again, as in the mid-career stage, many officers will remain indefinitely at class 2 or class 1. Within three years of his advancement to the senior level, every officer should be assigned to a year of education or other kind of broadening experience away from his work. The nature of training at this level can and should vary according to the merits of the individual case.

PROMOTIONS

Recommendation 22

Promotion from the junior to the mid-career stage, and from the mid-career to the senior stage, should be regarded as the pivotal points of a foreign affairs career. Officers should be "selected-into" succeeding stages only after especially intensive review and evaluation.

The promotional system is obviously of great importance in moving the foregoing proposals concerning career stages and career lines from the conceptual to the real. The Committee proposes, as a key principle, that the three career stages should be clearly distinguished by intensive review and evaluation of every officer prior to his selection into class 5 (the mid-career stage) and prior to his selection into class 2 (the senior officer stage).

Promotions of junior officers. The central staffs in charge of managing the junior officer programs should give regular attention not only to guiding and overseeing on-the-job training assignments but also to continuous assessment of the capabilities and potential of junior officers. There remains a need, however, for an objective review panel to make recommendations with regard to promotion of such officers from class 8 to 7, from 7 to 6, and from 6 to 5. The Committee suggests that a permanent review board be established for this purpose, and that officers be promoted whenever they merit it instead of in one large annual list. As indicated earlier, promotions through these junior grades should be rapid; evaluation reports by their supervising officers should be required at least every six months; and complete information should be readied for intensive review by the junior officer panelists prior to promotion from class 6 to class 5. At this stage, the panel should have available the entire record with regard to each officer, including all his evaluation reports, and should make use of other sources of information, inquiries, and consultations, as desirable. The panel should also be empowered to recommend selection-out of those officers who have failed to evidence growth potential or who otherwise do not appear promising, or, in doubtful cases, to recommend additional service at class 6. The review process should be thorough enough to provide basic guidance for the career development unit with regard to the officer's subsequent development. This would include, among other things, an indication of the nature of any special training the officer should receive and the types of work assignments for which he appears best fitted.

Promotions to class 2. A similarly intensive review process should take place at the stage of selection into the senior officer level. Here again, a continuing promotion panel would be desirable, and the investigation of each officer should be exhaustive. Not only would these panels have the complete record and all the evaluations on each officer, but special evaluation forms should be devised for obtaining more specific information and recommendations as to qualifications for serving at high executive and at expert levels. These panels should also be free to conduct special inquiries and consultations about individual officers.

This review should identify officers who ought to enter the executive career line as well as highly qualified specialists who warrant the top professional posts in the agency. It should be borne in mind that the levels of class 2 and above in the foreign affairs services are roughly equivalent to supergrades in the Civil Service and to General officers in the military service. Those who are performing adequately at class 3, but who do not show promise for the top executive and specialists posts would simply be retained without promotion. Those whose records revealed substandard or marginal abilities would be encouraged to retire or be selected-out.

PROMOTIONS WITHIN THE MID-CAREER AND SENIOR OFFICER STAGES

Recommendation 23

The panels established to recommend promotions from one class to the next higher one, up to class 1, should be guided generally by estimates of current and future requirements of specialized functional and area needs; and the makeup and procedures of such panels should be so devised as to assure equitable competition among officers in different specialized fields.

The imbalance among different specialized fields in the Department of State—the severe shortages in some and the surpluses in others—is demonstrated in the results of its promotion system. It may well be that its principal *cause* lies in the promotion system. There are many more political officers than needed; there are severe shortages of officers in administrative, economic, intelligence, and other fields. Yet the opinion is widespread that the best way to get ahead in the

Foreign Service is in political work. The evidence from the recommendations of recent selection boards (which recommend promotions) is either that this opinion is in fact true or that the better officers gravitate to political work, or, very probably, some of both. For example, in the 1960 rankings of selection boards, about five times as many officers with both a political and geographic specialization appeared in the highest 10 per cent as in the lowest. In contrast, almost twice as many specialized administrative officers and intelligence research officers appeared in the lowest tenth as in the highest.

One reason for this situation is that there is no clear-cut relationship between who is promoted and the needs of the organization in terms of specialist qualifications. Unlike most other organizations, public and private, the Foreign Service ranks all officers against one another according to highly generalized criteria and without specific regard to Department needs at each successively higher level. The Committee believes that, through the manpower planning and career development activities discussed earlier in this report, broad guidelines as to needs by specialty can be developed. These should provide the promotion panels with general directions, not specific quotas, to consider in their promotion determinations.

A second problem lies in the difficulty, if not the impossibility, of ranking officers against others with widely differing types of responsibilities. The problems of comparing—and placing in rank order of superiority and inferiority—several hundred different individuals working in Washington and at posts all over the world, on the basis only of the written record and the evaluations of others, are great enough. Adding to these a wide disparity of duties of the different officers—some visa specialists, some budget officers, some reporters on economic developments, some negotiators of international agreements, and a great many others—makes the task of ranking very nearly metaphysical. In the face of such problems, it was probably inevitable that some highly generalized criteria as to what constitutes a "good" Foreign Service Officer would become the dominant, if not the exclusive, yardstick.

The Committee believes that specific recognition and evaluation of competence in specialized fields should be built into the organization and operations of the promotion panels. Each such board for each class of officers should include both private and public members, and each should include persons accomplished in the major functional fields of the agency. The board should be divided into sub-panels, one for each major functional field or cluster of related fields. The sub-panels would make the initial review of officers within each primary functional field, comparing economic officers to economic officers, administrative officers to administrative officers, and so forth. Each sub-panel would classify the officers under review into four groups: (1) those who merit promotion, listed in rank order, (2) those whose performance is so marginal as to warrant consideration for selection-out, (3) those not yet ready for promotion, but whose performance is regarded as competent, and (4) those whom the sub-panel decides it is not competent to review (such as the officer so new to the field that it would not be fair to compare his functional performance to the performance of others with longer experience). The entire panel would review the recommendations of the sub-panels and would make final recommendations relative to promotion, selection-out, and retention. In this second of the two steps, the more general qualities and total achievements of the officers under consideration would be considered along with functional proficiency.

The pattern and procedure proposed above should apply equally to USIA and AID. The former agency now uses a system essentially similar to that of the Department of State. In recent years, AID promotions have been determined by completely functionalized panels, one for each of sixteen different functional fields. The panel and sub-panel machinery here suggested would provide across-the-board comparison on general qualities in addition to the strictly occupational competition heretofore provided in AID.

PROMOTIONS TO CAREER MINISTER AND CAREER AMBASSADOR

Recommendation 24

The ranks of career minister and career ambassador should be open to qualified career officers in AID and USIA. Recommendations for promotions to these ranks should be made by the Board of Foreign Affairs Personnel to the Secretary of State before submission to the President. Experience in at least two foreign affairs agencies should become a normal qualification for such promotions.

This recommendation is the capstone of the Committee's concepts of a family of services and compatible personnel structures and its emphasis on the need to broaden the base for selection of executive talent. The career officer in USIA or AID should be able to aspire to the rank of career minister just as does the career officer in the Department of State. The designation that positions are of comparable importance to that of a chief of diplomatic mission, and the nomination of individuals to the President for appointment as career ministers, should remain subject to the approval of the Secretary of State. Inasmuch as career ambassadors are selected exclusively

91

from among career ministers, officers of USIA and AID who attain the latter rank may also aspire to the higher one if they are qualified.

PERFORMANCE EVALUATION

Recommendation 25

An improved system for evaluating employee performance and capabilities should be devised. It should recognize the several management purposes to be served and should be related to the career stages through which officers will progress. The basic elements of the system should apply uniformly among the three foreign affairs agencies.

The evaluation of employees in terms of their performance and capabilities is especially important in a mobile career service where rank applies to the man and employees are assigned on a worldwide basis, are promoted on the basis of competitive merit, and are subject to selection-out. Personnel decisions vital to the individual and to the agency are made repeatedly on the basis of the cumulative written performance record.

The importance of performance evaluation is matched only by its difficulty. The Committee knows of no single system that will satisfy the basic purposes that underlie the evaluation of employees and at the same time successfully exclude the frailties of human judgment.

Without losing sight of the limitations inherent in any evaluation system, the Committee suggests that one suitable for foreign affairs career personnel should emphasize the following basic purposes: (1) to provide an orderly way for the individual employee to assess his past performance and future potential; (2) to encourage supervisors to help their subordinates raise the level of their performance and usefulness; and (3) to provide management with a cumulative flow of objective information regarding employee performance and capabilities which it can use in making decisions in such matters as promotion, assignment, training, and selection-out.

The Committee recognizes that the foreign affairs agencies strive continually to improve the quality and usefulness of performance-evaluation reports. But it believes that the existing systems can be improved in a number of respects.

1. Although Foreign Service performance reports contain much useful information, the typical report gives insufficient attention to the officer's competence in the particular function in which he is engaged. General qualities such as cooperativeness, tact, initiative,

and resourcefulness tend to be weighted out of proportion to the performance requirements of particular types of job responsibilities.

2. Another problem arises from the paucity of common rating standards for different kinds of jobs against which tò appraise individual performance and potential. The Committee is under no illusion that, in a field as complex and diverse as foreign affairs, precise standards of performance can take the place of sound individual judgment. At the same time, however, it suggests that a concerted effort be made to provide rating officers with more clearly defined standards of performance in different activities and at different grade levels.

3. The use of numerical ratings to indicate degrees of excellence or inadequacy has been of little value, since rating officers tend to rate most employees within too narrow a range, and usually near the top. The selection boards which recommend promotions, moreover, find it exceedingly difficult to distinguish among officers when reports are over-generalized and devoid of supporting facts and concrete examples.

4. More important than these, however, is the fact that the present rating form attempts to serve too many different purposes. Appraisal of growth potential, training needed, fitness for promotion, or suitable next assignment, for example, while related to evaluaation of a person's performance on a particular job, involve consideration of additional factors.

The Committee suggests that the three agencies collaborate in developing an improved performance-evaluation system that will give greater emphasis to assessing functional competence, provide rating officers with more definitive guides as to what constitutes an acceptable standard of performance, place a premium on straightforward and factually supported supervisory appraisals, and develop different rating instruments—one, for example, for evaluating job performance and general qualifications for service, and another for evaluating potential, fitness for promotion, need for training, and related matters.

As noted earlier, the evaluation system should be related to the career stages. Junior officer evaluation reports should stress such factors as adaptability, motivation, leadership qualities, career potential, and other more general aspects of service suitability, as well as functional competence. At the mid-career stage, while evaluation of functional competence should be given strong emphasis, it is also important to watch for and report on supervisory and executive qualities. At the senior levels, appraisals should focus principally on management and executive skills, comprehension and breadth of understanding of foreign affairs, and depth and breadth of functional expertise, where appropriate.

There has been controversy over whether or not the statutory provision, enacted in 1955, permitting Foreign Service personnel to see all or any part of their efficiency records has impaired the objectivity of ratings. The Committee's study of pre- and post-1955 reports shows no measurable change in the severity of numerical ratings and narrative content.

The Committee believes that those aspects of evaluation which reflect the supervisor's responsibility for telling employees how well they are performing their jobs and otherwise meeting general standards of service should be freely discussed with the employee, made a part of his personnel record, and be open to his inspection. This purpose cannot be achieved through a system of "secret" ratings.

Those aspects of evaluation which relate to growth potential, promotability, reassignment by reason of family problems, selection for advanced training, as examples, though properly a part of the personnel record, need not be disclosed by the supervisor. Like other aspects of the personnel file, however, they could be disclosed to the employee by the central personnel office upon request.

ASSIGNMENTS

The Committee has already touched upon various aspects of assignment and utilization of personnel, particularly in Chapter III and in its discussion of career development. It may be useful to restate and amplify some of these concepts in terms of assignment policy for professional career personnel.

It is important that foreign service personnel serve a significant portion of their careers in the United States. While flexibility in length of overseas tours is essential, officers should normally be returned for a "home" assignment after not more than eight years of service abroad.

Overseas tours of duty must be flexible in order to take into account hardship conditions, need for continuity, area specialization, family problems, home-leave eligibility, and a host of other factors. In general, the Committee endorses the objective of longer tours of duty at a particular post, ranging in unusual instances up to as long as six or eight years. All officers serving abroad, including area specialists, should be reassigned to another geographic area as needed to preserve objectivity and perspective.

Assignment policies should reflect the requirements of the three career stages. Tours of duty of junior officers, for example, should be comparatively short in order to provide a variety of functional and area experience, including at least brief exposure to the work of one of the other foreign affairs agencies. At the mid-career level, assignment should stress functional experience and area expertise. But if the development of executive potential is to be fostered at this stage, the assignment process should provide an officer with at least one opportunity to gain experience in and demonstrate his talent for supervision and executive responsibility. At the senior levels, assignment policy should provide further broadening of experience and optimum use of executive talent and functional expertise.

The Committee also stresses the importance of assignments outside an officer's own agency. Interagency assignments should be a frequent occurrence within the family of services; and, on a selected basis, temporary service with such other bodies as the Departments of Defense, Treasury, Commerce, and Labor should be encouraged. More attention should be paid to occasional assignments to international organizations, private American business, and labor organizations.

Rotational on-the-job training assignments of junior officers should be controlled almost exclusively by the staffs in charge of junior officer programs. At mid-career and above, operating bureaus obviously have a much larger stake in utilization of personnel, yet basic authority must be retained by central personnel offices in assigning officers across bureau lines and in specifying training to meet over-all manpower requirements. The Committee believes that the strengthened career development programs will be an important tool in helping to strike a balance between immediate and long-range needs. The recommendation in each officer's career plan should largely determine the operating bureau to which he is assigned on promotion to class 5; the bureau would then have authority for specific utilization of the officer consistent with the projected career plan. Thereafter, the career development units should be authorized to recommend reassignments to other bureaus, to training, or to other agencies as the officer progresses and as his career plan is revised. There would still be a need for decision-making panels, such as now exist in the Department of State and USIA, to review proposals for reassignment. However, the enlarged role of the career development unit and other concepts proposed in this chapter should greatly ease the tremendous burdens presently resting on these panels. These comments are directed primarily to the mid-career stage; at senior levels, career planning becomes less of a factor, and the agencies should continue to use executive assignment committees for both operating and training assignments.

The above comments are not stated in the form of a recommendation but rather as lending encouragement to efforts that have already begun along the lines indicated. There is one aspect of assignment policy, however, concerning which the Committee wishes to make a specific recommendation.

Recommendation 26

The senior executive officers of the foreign affairs agencies should constitute a pool of talent for key executive jobs to the maximum extent consistent with the retention of control and action responsibility by the agency heads. In filling such posts, the agency heads should draw on rosters to be developed by the Board of Foreign Affairs Personnel.

The Board of Foreign Affairs Personnel should systematically review the records of officers advanced to executive positions by each agency, for the purpose of drawing up qualifying lists to be used in making interagency assignments at the senior levels and in staffing top-ranking positions both at home and abroad. While the qualifying lists would be considered by agency heads as advisory only, the Committee believes that the arrangement envisioned would exert a significant influence over time. It would encourage interagency assignments; provide an enlarged reservoir from which to draw executive talent; open up opportunities for some exceptionally talented persons; and bring about closer coordination of the three foreign affairs agencies at the top.

SELECTION-OUT
Recommendation 27

All the foreign affairs agencies should have selection-out authority, but selection-out for time in class should be eliminated.

The Committee's concept of career stages, most importantly the intensive review processes before officers are advanced to classes 5 and 2, affects selection-out as much as other aspects of managing a career service. For one thing, a great deal more emphasis is placed on the positive idea of "selection-in" than on the negative one of "selection-out." Secondly, the thrust of the Committee's recommendations would concentrate selection-out at the two points where least damage would be done to the individual.

The "up or out" idea behind the present promotion and selection-out system for Foreign Service Officers in the Department of State has had a rocky history. The system has been used gingerly, the ground rules have shifted, and the differential treatment of some specialists has given rise to serious questions about its fairness. Yet, some kind of selection-out provision is essential for managing and keeping vital a mobile career system based on the rank-in-man concept. Therefore, the Committee proposes extending selection-out authority to all foreign affairs agencies on a uniform basis.

The time-in-class provision for selection-out of Foreign Service Officers has not been an effective means of weeding out "deadwood." Between January 1, 1957, and July 1, 1962, only 12 officers were selected-out on the basis of time in class without promotion, and only 7 more would have been had they not also been required to retire because of age or disability. The time-in-class provision has had a damaging effect in that it has put pressure on promotion panels to advance some people who should not have been promoted in order to "save" them from selection-out—the so-called "tombstone" promotions.

Selection-out of seasoned personnel in their middle years is a difficult, unkind, and often brutal business under any circumstances. Furthermore, it is extravagant to dismiss a man who is performing competently, even though he does not merit promotion to the next higher grade. Selection-out should normally be limited to those who are inadequate or of marginal competence. This would apply at any grade level, but the Committee's recommendations would concentrate most selections-out in the two thorough review processes on entry into the mid-career and senior levels. A person selected-out during or at the end of probationary status will be young enough to begin a new career. At the senior level, the main purpose of the review process is to identify officers capable of filling expert or command positions at higher grades. Many officers not selected for these levels would be performing competently at their present level and would remain there. At the same time, however, the process would also identify officers whose contributions to the service are, for all intents and purposes, at an end. Selection-out of these officers at this relatively senior level would be greatly eased by the fact that they would normally be eligible for retirement with an immediate or early annuity.

Selection-out provides an effective means of administering a reduction in force should that become necessary. The Committee suggests that the legislation authorizing selection-out provide for its use for this purpose notwithstanding any other law, subject to provision for administrative appeal. In the case of a reduction in force, appropriate consideration should be given to both length and quality of service.

The Committee believes that selection-out should apply initially to the career professional officers in the respective foreign services of the three agencies. In principle, the Committee favors extending selection-out to the personnel now in the Civil Service and to Staff officers, but it recognizes that this step must be taken in conjunction with appropriate revision of retirement provisions and severance benefits. Selection-out is not needed in the case of Reserve personnel in view of the nature of their appointments.

OUT-PLACEMENT

Recommendation 28

Provision should be made in each agency to assist employees who are involuntarily separated to find other employment.

The enforced separation of employees due to selection-out, reduction in force, completion of overseas assignments (especially for AID technicians), health problems, mandatory retirement, and other related causes places an obligation on the foreign affairs agencies to assist these employees to obtain employment elsewhere. This is particularly important in the case of overseas personnel who are out of touch with employment opportunities in the United States. Government agencies generally provide such out-placement assistance only when there is a reduction in force that affects relatively large numbers of satisfactory employees who are separated through no fault of their own. The Committee would extend this concept to the various other circumstances that result in the involuntary separation of personnel. There may well be an increase of movement in and out of the foreign affairs agencies as new specialized needs develop and as closer relationships are built with outside professional fields. This heightens the need for a continuing out-placement service.

RETIREMENT

Recommendation 29

Officers in the career foreign services of USIA and AID should be placed under the Foreign Service Retirement System.* Legislation applicable to that system should be amended to provide for automatic adjustments of annuities based on increased costs of living. Greater use should be made of the administrative discretion authorized under existing legislation to extend the mandatory retirement age.

---

*In addition, Foreign Service Staff personnel with ten years of overseas service should, of course, be included, as they are in the Department of State. See Chapter III for a brief discussion concerning retirement provisions for the headquarters or departmental personnel of the foreign affairs agencies.

The establishment of parallel and substantially equal foreign services for information and development officers necessitates the extension of the Foreign Service Retirement System to accommodate them on an equal basis with Foreign Service Officers.

ADJUSTMENT OF ANNUITIES OF RETIRED PERSONNEL

Recently enacted legislation authorizes automatic adjustments in the annuities of persons retired under the Civil Service Retirement System based on increased living costs.* The Committee endorses the Department of State's request for legislation that will provide similar authorization in the administration of the Foreign Service Retirement System.

MANDATORY RETIREMENT FOR AGE

Most Foreign Service Officers must retire at 60. (The principal exceptions are officers with the rank of career minister or career ambassador, who must retire at 65.) The Secretary of State may at his discretion extend an officer's service in the public interest up to an additional five years—that is, to age 65—but he has rarely done so. The mandatory retirement age of 60 is relatively young compared with age provisions of most retirement plans, both public and private. For example, mandatory retirement age under the Civil Service system is 70 years with a minimum of fifteen years of service. This system applies to USIA and AID personnel, including those in the foreign services of those agencies, as well as to most Foreign Service Staff personnel of the State Department.

One reason for this age limitation on length of service in the Foreign Service was to encourage attrition at the top and thereby enhance promotional opportunities of those coming up the line. It was also designed in recognition of careers spent largely in foreign countries. The situation today is changed in both respects. The Foreign Service Officer Corps is much larger today than was envisaged fifteen years ago. It provides many more opportunities for advancement to an exceptionally high proportion of top-level executive posts. Foreign Service Officers can expect to serve in the United States for substantial portions of their careers. The Foreign Service includes, and will continue to include, many officers of distinction and value who will not attain the rank of career minister. Mandatory retirement annually deprives the Service of a number of officers at or near the peaks of their careers; this is illustrated by the highly responsible positions in other organizations which many retired Foreign Service Officers are asked to fill.

---

*Public Law 87-793, 87th Congress, October 11, 1962.

The State Department has instituted no regular procedure to make positive use of the Secretary's discretionary authority to extend an officer's service beyond the age of 60. This problem will become more serious when the Foreign Service Retirement System is extended to the career foreign service personnel of USIA and AID. Both of these agencies now employ a number of highly competent officers older than 60.

Consequently, the Committee recommends that full and positive use be made of the discretionary authority referred to above in order to retain the services of able officers. A systematic procedure should be established for reviewing the qualifications of all officers approaching mandatory retirement age in the light of projected personnel needs. Those whose services are needed should be retained for periods up to an additional five years.

EQUALIZATION OF BENEFITS OF OVERSEAS EMPLOYEES

The Committee has emphasized the need for substantial uniformity of personnel policies and equality in conditions of service applicable to employees of the three principal foreign affairs agencies. Its recommendations concerning personnel categories, appointment, commissioning, promotion, provision of a uniform salary schedule, and extension of the Foreign Service Retirement System to the career foreign services of USIA and AID are in furtherance of this objective. The Committee also proposes that the Board of Foreign Affairs Personnel work toward the removal of unwarranted disparities in benefits accorded the agencies' overseas personnel.

Recommendation 30

Differences in benefits accorded overseas employees of comparable rank and responsibility in the different foreign affairs agencies should be eliminated to the maximum practicable extent.

The effective conduct of our foreign affairs depends upon the Government's ability to recruit and retain able people who are prepared to serve abroad, often under difficult and trying circumstances. Over the course of the past decade, there has been substantial improvement in the benefits accorded employees of the foreign affairs agencies and their families. Generally speaking, overseas allowances, salary differentials for hardship-post service, and medical benefits now apply uniformly to the various categories of foreign affairs employees. Despite this favorable trend, there is still considerable disparity in benefits among personnel categories and among the foreign affairs agencies themselves. Relatively few of these differences are attributable to legislative provisions; some are based on long-established precedent and generally accepted international custom and practice; others reflect differences in agency policies; still others derive from insufficiencies in support funds for overseas personnel.

In surveying many overseas missions, the Committee was struck by the need for a greater degree of uniform practice than presently exists. For example, the Committee found that one agency provides official transportation to convey employees, including those with private automobiles, to and from work, whereas another agency at the same post requires that employees who have their own cars provide their own means of conveyance. At a tropical post, one agency provides the homes of its personnel with one air conditioner, while a second agency furnishes two, and a third furnishes none. Disparities that might provoke only moderate irritation at home seem far more important abroad, where employees and their families sometimes must be relatively isolated from the society in which they live. Public servants overseas are far more dependent on their employer than those at home in regard to such important matters as housing, educational facilities for their children, food, local transportation, and a host of others. Different treatment by different agencies at the same post magnifies incipient problems of morale and interagency friction and thus can do great damage to the spirit of the "country team."

While the Committee has not made an extensive study of the subject of fringe benefits and perquisites, it is satisfied that much can be done to alleviate some of the existing difficulties.

1. Legislative authority and funds should be provided to enable the Secretary of State to establish, maintain, and operate schools abroad for dependents of United States citizens employees. Although the Act for International Development and other legislation make it possible for the Government to provide such educational facilities or assist in their support, this authority is not available to the State Department. This lack is particularly important in certain areas of the world, a prime example being the Eastern European posts, which are especially demanding on employees and their families. The Committee endorses the expansion of State Department authority in this field which was proposed to Congress in 1962.

2. Interagency efforts are now under way to standardize regulations and practices relative to transportation of effects, modes of travel and travel allowances, payment of per diem, and others. These

efforts should be extended to cover the full range of benefits that can be standardized by administrative action. The Committee believes that a more consistent and uniform policy should be followed with respect to provision of Government-owned, Government-leased, and privately leased housing, maintenance services, furnishing of household equipment, commissaries, and other related forms of support, with due regard to local conditions.

3. The Committee hopes that a fresh approach can be made to the difficult problem of diplomatic titles which carry concomitant benefits, privileges, and status recognition. The need for diplomatic status should be a function principally of the nature of responsibility assigned to an individual rather than of the agency by which he is employed.* Chiefs of diplomatic missions should determine which positions occupied by United States citizen personnel in their countries require diplomatic status, taking into account local considerations. Their determinations should be consistent with more general standards that take into account the needs and interests of the several agencies as well as generally accepted international practice.

4. Regulations and practices relating to conditions of service must keep pace with changing needs and circumstances, including availability of funds. The Committee has been amazed, nonetheless, by the constantly shifting character and pace of regulatory changes, revisions, freezes, restrictions, removals of restrictions, postponements, cancellations, and renewals. Most employees doubtless accept this circumstance as one of the vagaries of public service. It seems evident to the Committee, however, that a constantly shifting base can only detract from an organization's effectiveness. Improved systems of forward programing and budgeting would greatly alleviate this situation.

5. The Board of Foreign Affairs Personnel, under the proposed Executive Under Secretary, should supervise continuing efforts to equalize and stabilize practices in these regards.

The foregoing suggestions have been directed specifically to the three foreign affairs agencies within the Committee's terms of reference. As rapidly as possible, measures should be undertaken to equalize benefits among overseas personnel of other Government agencies as well.

---

*This matter has been discussed briefly in Chapter III.

VIII

EDUCATION

AND TRAINING

FOR THE

NEW

DIPLOMACY

*"No one in these times can go far on
the intellectual capital he acquires
in youth.
Unless he keeps his knowledge
or skill up to date, revises it, adds
to it, enriches it with experience,
and supplements it with new ideas
as they displace the old, he is soon
handicapped for the duties
of the day."*

ROBERT D. CALKINS

SUMMARY

Given the dynamic world setting in which foreign affairs personnel must operate, opportunities for training and continuing professional education should equal the best available to any profession. This is not now the case. In order to strengthen the professional qualifications of foreign affairs personnel:

- the quantity of training and education available to foreign affairs personnel should be increased, and its quality should be elevated;
- a new and highest-quality National Foreign Affairs College should be established to offer appropriate courses at advanced levels and to provide the institutional coordination and direction for foreign affairs training programs, whether pursued in governmental or non-governmental agencies;
- administrative machinery should be developed for the projection of training requirements for the foreign affairs agencies;
- professional training and education programs, whether offered by government or private institutions, should be planned and meshed with projected patterns of career growth.

THE DEGREE OF COMPETENCE an officer brings to a job in the field of foreign affairs depends on four major ingredients: (1) his native endowment; (2) his education and experience prior to entry; (3) his experience after he enters the service; and (4) his training and education after initial appointment.

Of these, the first two have been discussed in Chapter VI in connection with recruitment and selection. The third hinges on the successive assignments of officers within their services. It also depends on the seriousness and effectiveness with which supervising officers guide and instruct their subordinates; this is, indeed, a major responsibility of all intermediate and senior officers. In the long pull, the best of all teachers is experience on the job, but its usefulness depends on the educational foundation the officer brings to his work, especially his professional training and education after initial appointment.

This last-named ingredient requires particular attention in foreign affairs for the following reasons:

First, universities do not provide specific professional preparation embracing the totality of foreign affairs work. This represents a notable contrast with well-established professions like law, medicine, and business administration whose graduate schools not only provide specific professional preparation but also maintain contact with, and interest in, the professionals they have graduated.

Second, increased specialization (which has already been described as characteristic of a modern foreign affairs establishment) necessitates continuing programs of high-level professional training. On the one hand, professional specialization—in economics, political analysis, communications, and science, among others—requires sustained contact with other professionals in universities, research institutions, and government agencies; a specialist can quickly become out of date without the intellectual nourishment that comes from periodic exposure to those who are adding to the content of his field. On the other hand, those who become eligible for the higher executive posts will increasingly be drawn from specialized careers, and will require advanced programs to allow them to review the broad picture of national diplomacy and strategy.

INCREASE IN TRAINING PROGRAMS GENERALLY
Recommendation 31

Opportunities and programs for training and further education of professional foreign affairs personnel, both through governmental and outside institutions, should be substantially enlarged.

Most professions today recognize the need for continuing or periodic training of their practitioners, and in none is the argument more cogent than for foreign affairs personnel, operating as they do in a context of complexity and rapid change, and working, as so many of them must, thousands of miles from their home bases. It is the opinion of the Committee that the truly professional nature of this work, and the educational requirements that accompany it, are inadequately recognized in present training programs.

The seriousness of the training deficit among the foreign affairs agencies is suggested by the proportion of officer time dedicated to training in relation to officer time *in toto*. Among the United States Information Agency Reserve Officers, this proportion is slightly over 2 per cent; in the Agency for International Development, including its participating agency personnel, it is about the same; among Foreign Service Officers and Reserve Officers in the Department of State, it is about 5 per cent. The comparable figure in the military departments is roughly 12 per cent.*

Among the academic fraternity, one year in six or seven is considered proper for sabbatical leave for research and further education. A goal of one year in ten would not appear unreasonable for professionals in the field of foreign affairs, exclusive of language "tool" training. This would have the effect, among the foreign services of the three agencies, of doubling the total amount of training, other than in languages, in the State Department and quadrupling it in both AID and USIA.

A NATIONAL FOREIGN AFFAIRS COLLEGE AT THE GRADUATE LEVEL

Recommendation 32

There should be established, under the highest auspices and leadership, a National Foreign Affairs College which would provide inservice training at an advanced level for professional personnel. It would replace the Foreign Service Institute.

Several problems arise from the organizational cleavages among the different training institutions. Except in the field of languages, the Foreign Service Institute is widely regarded as primarily for the training of Foreign Service Officers of the State Department. USIA and AID have each developed their own training programs. All are, to a degree, parochial. None is well equipped to consider United States

---

*These figures exclude language training.

105

policy as a unity, and to relate its parts and its specialties to those of the others. With the present organizational division, great opportunities are lost for sharing experiences, for exchanging and challenging points of view, for learning the problems not only of one's own job but those of others in related programs. The training structure is a roadblock, rather than an avenue, to the realization of a true family of services. And the Foreign Service Institute has found it difficult to embrace the full dimensions of the new diplomacy as described in earlier chapters of this report.

The time is ripe for a new training institution of the highest quality to serve the needs of the Department of State, USIA, AID, and, as deemed appropriate, other agencies of the Federal Government with foreign affairs responsibilities. The Committee suggests that this institution, which should offer courses only at an advanced level, be known as the National Foreign Affairs College. It should enjoy the maximum of freedom in its staffing, work, and internal management that is consistent with the maintenance of necessary executive supervision. The National Foreign Affairs College should be located in or near Washington and should be housed in its own building, designed and constructed for its special needs. Such a building would be a symbol of the importance of foreign affairs and of public concern for the systematic strengthening of officers engaged in this work.

The National Foreign Affairs College should be the primary professional and language training institution for foreign affairs personnel. The majority of its trainees would be from the State Department, AID, and USIA, but it should also be open to trainees from other civilian and military agencies having staffs concerned with foreign affairs programs, as appropriate.

The National Foreign Affairs College should be a semi-autonomous educational institution. Its integrity of purpose and performance from the beginning should be protected against the claims of partisanship, special interests, or other damaging interventions; this goal would be a particular responsibility of its governing officials. Basic policy direction should be provided by a Board of Trustees, appointed by the President and including both Government officials and public members of outstanding civic and academic reputation. Executive leadership should be vested in a Chancellor, nominated by the Board and appointed by the President. He should be a person of recognized attainment.

The College should have its own separate appropriation for administrative costs, including faculty salaries, physical plant, and other facilities. The salaries of all employees enrolled as trainees should be paid by their respective agencies.

The basic purposes of the National Foreign Affairs College would be:

1. To provide a visible and recognized center for the planning and coordination of education and training and for the conduct of certain advanced professional instruction programs geared to the needs of foreign affairs officers.
2. To provide an institution where, and a climate in which, officers of the Department of State, AID, USIA, and other agencies as appropriate, could meet to explore the common and the special elements of their problems and to learn how better to relate their various efforts and skills to each other.
3. To work persistently to improve the curriculum of training courses. To this end, research and updating of instructional materials and methods are vital. The present high level of the Foreign Service Institute language program, which should become an element of the College, is a striking example of the success that high-quality research can bring to a training program. The faculty of the College should apply this lesson in other areas—for example, by developing case studies of foreign affairs decision-making, analytical memoranda on foreign affairs issues, studies of the interaction of the public and private sectors of the economy in the conduct of foreign affairs, and full-length studies of problem areas in United States foreign affairs, distilling from history the lessons of successful and unsuccessful experiences.
4. The National Foreign Affairs College should provide leadership, guidance, and assistance to the training staffs of the foreign affairs agencies, including the training programs conducted at overseas posts.
5. The College should also maintain liaison with private research and educational institutions in the foreign affairs fields, and with private businesses and other organizations operating in the international field.

FACULTY

The National Foreign Affairs College will require a teaching staff with special characteristics that stem from its character as a professional college which must meet the training requirements of a complex profession.

There should be a small, permanent core faculty made up of persons who have that rare mixture of high academic standards and rich exposure to the practical world of foreign affairs. Fortunately, during World War II many university men were drawn into public and foreign affairs and they, and others who followed them, have managed to bridge the worlds of the campus and the Government. Able men of this type are in short supply, and the College will have to create an environment in which the best of them will wish to work and where others, deficient in either academic or Government background, can receive the requisite experience. In addition, the College will need a permanent staff of professional linguists for language instruction.

This core faculty should be supplemented by specialists selected from the staffs of Government agencies and assigned to the College for appropriate tours of duty. Some retiring career ambassadors or ministers could probably be persuaded to spend a year in residence to lend the weight of their experience to the programs of the College.

Finally, the faculty should also include visiting professors, drawn from leading colleges and universities, on leave for one to three years' service with the National Foreign Affairs College. These faculty members would bring to the College the broad perspective and high specialization that the best American scholarship represents. Further, they would benefit from exposure to the more practical orientation of the Government and foreign affairs officers who would also be in residence for tours of duty. Indeed, it may be that not the least important consequence of the establishment of this National Foreign Affairs College would be the creation of an effective link between the world of scholarship and the world of practical experience in foreign affairs, to the mutual stimulation and benefit of both.

RELATIONS WITH UNIVERSITIES AND COLLEGES

In performing as a liaison agency with the universities and other institutions concerned with foreign affairs training and research, the College should concentrate on the following tasks: providing a center of information concerning university programs of training and research; advising the foreign affairs agencies on university assignments for their personnel; arranging for such assignments as appropriate and evaluating their effectiveness; and stimulating and lending support and advice to the universities in the development of their programs relevant to foreign affairs.

The College should develop standards for a division of responsibility between the College and the universities. In so doing, the College should recognize that it cannot, and should not, attempt to duplicate the rich and varied resources of the nation's educational institutions; instead, its task is to relate its efforts to existing resources, to utilize them and to supplement them as necessary.

In the main, the universities should be the place of training when:

1. educational experience requiring a considerable length of time is needed—a full academic year or more (except for intensive training in the difficult languages and in certain other instances as suggested below); or
2. educational experience in an established discipline is needed— as in economics, political science, international law, history, sociology, or the physical sciences; or
3. renewed exposure to the variety of academic life, away from the Governmental setting, is considered a valuable part of the education needed.

Correspondingly, the National Foreign Affairs College should provide the training when:
1. training closely geared to ongoing foreign affairs problems and methods is needed; or
2. when exposure to the variety of viewpoints represented by personnel from diverse foreign affairs agencies is considered a valuable part of the individual's development; or
3. training heavily dependent on information not available to university staffs is needed; or
4. emergency training for which university staffs are not equipped is needed; or
5. short-term training (including most orientation courses), which would disrupt university time schedules, is needed.

The College should offer some courses of up to a year in duration such as the Senior Seminar in Foreign Policy presently given by the Foreign Service Institute. Consideration should also be given to mixed offerings in which part of the work would be taken outside the Government, followed by integrating seminars at the College.

TRAINING WITHIN THE FOREIGN AFFAIRS AGENCIES

Just as the National Foreign Affairs College should not attempt to duplicate university training resources, so also it should not attempt to absorb all the training activities of the foreign affairs agencies. The College should be a professional-level training institution. In general, non-professional and routine staff training should remain with the agencies. Each agency may properly wish to conduct part of the orientation training for professional staff, and each may also need to administer some specialized courses for its own professional staff when unique agency problems and methods are the dominant training need. In general, training courses and programs dealing with procedures, methods, and activities unique to particular groups of personnel in the foreign affairs field should continue to be performed within the training offices of the appropriate agency.

TRAINING NEEDS AND TRAINING PLANS

Recommendation 33

On the basis of forward manpower plans provided by the agencies, the National Foreign Affairs College, as well as the training divisions in each agency, should systematically develop and coordinate plans for individual training programs. The College should establish machinery whereby appropriate training courses, wherever taught, can be regularly evaluated; present and anticipated needs of the agencies can be consolidated and correlated; and plans for new or revised courses can be developed in response to such needs, whether at the College or elsewhere.

As indicated in earlier chapters, none of the agencies has yet developed a manpower planning system adequate to permit the projection of training requirements far into the future. None has made truly effective a career planning system for individual officers within which training assignments could be firmly predicted and scheduled. Hit-or-miss training programs have been the rule. Aside from the orientation and language programs, many of the courses have been developed in response to *ad hoc* problems and pressures, sometimes arising from outside agencies, the White House, or the Congress.

Training programs should be conceived as integral elements of manpower development and should be responsive to the best possible judgments of future manpower needs. Fundamental guidance should derive from the agencies themselves, but the National Foreign Affairs College should consolidate and coordinate such information and from it develop over-all training plans. Furthermore, the College will be in a strategic position to anticipate and respond to needs arising from new situations and developments, many of which should provide the basis for formal training efforts. Its semi-independent status will enable it to assess and respond to needs common to all foreign affairs personnel, regardless of organizational attachment. An example of the kind of cross-organizational enterprise here envisioned is the Country-Team Seminar program, begun by the Foreign Service Institute in 1962 in response to a Presidential directive. In these seminars, senior personnel of the various agencies involved in country-team operations overseas studied such modern problems in United States diplomacy as counter-insurgency, economic development, and social reform in the developing countries.

There are a number of other subject-matter fields that the Committee feels have been relatively neglected in the training programs, or that warrant inclusion in new or existing courses. These areas include: *political analysis and reporting; economics,* including development economics, regional economic communities, the relationship of domestic and foreign economic policy, the nature of the free enterprise system, and international finance and monetary movements; *intelligence* machinery and methodology; *international organizations* and *multilateral negotiation; national security policy; science and foreign policy; social change* and *social reform; international communications; business* and its involvement in foreign affairs; and *executive development.*

Training needs of a somewhat different order would include: expanded programs of orientation for wives and dependents; training of professional departmental personnel; and orientation and training for contract and other short-term personnel in the foreign affairs agencies.

Recommendation 34

Training and education programs should be conceived and designed as integral elements of career development, and meshed with the stages in each officer's career, as outlined in Chapter VII.

Training programs must be considered in relation to the three principal stages of officer development, namely: for all junior officers of classes 8 through 6, a brief initial orientation course and periodic seminars in Washington and overseas; for all middle-level officers of classes 5 through 3, a basic officer course and specialized training as individually appropriate; and for all officers of class 2, command or expert training. It would be expected that before an officer is promoted to class 1 he would normally have had at least one year of advanced training at the level of the present Senior Seminar in Foreign Policy.

IX

NON-CAREER SPECIALISTS FOR OVERSEAS DEVELOPMENT

"Just as the development diplomat is a man with a vocation, so development diplomacy, if it is to succeed, must reflect a new sense of vocation in the West towards the historic transformation going on in the underdeveloped world."

EUGENE R. BLACK

SUMMARY

The achievement of United States objectives in helping the development of the less-privileged nations of the world depends heavily on the mobilization of our best professional resources. In order that the Agency for International Development may operate most effectively toward these goals, the Committee proposes that:

- development assistance policies be formulated for each overseas country, as a basis for estimating needs for specialized personnel in each subject-matter field;
- through a variety of devices, the problems of international development be built into the fabric of the various professions as an integral element and a major field in their educational programs, research, and practice;
- AID use the most appropriate means for recruiting and engaging the services of professionals in different fields, but that the majority be employed on a temporary and non-career basis;
- more attention be given to training development specialists prior to their overseas assignments.

THE ANNUAL DEBATE over how much will be appropriated for foreign aid has become a predictable phenomenon in the political calendar. It tends to overshadow, and also warp, the persistent personnel problems in technical assistance. These problems are in some ways more serious than the over-all amount of dollars; the effectiveness with which the use of the dollars is planned and with which they are actually expended is heavily contingent on the caliber of the people charged with these responsibilities. More than this, the direct help that professionally competent persons can render to developing countries is as important as the amount of grants and loans, though in dollar terms they account for less than one-tenth of total AID expenditures.

It is useful to consider the professional personnel engaged in overseas development work in three broad categories:

Development Planners and Managers: These comprise officers responsible for planning, negotiating, recommending, and, upon approval, administering with the host governments, development programs. They include the majority of AID's domestic professional personnel and, overseas, the mission directors, deputies, administrative officers, program officers, comptrollers, and a small group of specialists in such major professional fields as education, public health, and agriculture.

Development Advisers: These officers are professional specialists whose primary function is to advise host governments, AID development managers, and other organizations or institutions on specific country projects or aspects of projects within their fields of professional competence.

Development Operators and Assistants: These include professional and sub-professional personnel (teachers, well-drillers, and so forth) who are directly engaged in carrying out specific projects within approved development programs.

In earlier chapters of this report, the Committee has emphasized the need for a true career service for some of the professional staff of AID. In general, this service should comprehend those described here as development planners and managers. The principal concern of this chapter is the specialized personnel from a variety of professions who are and will be required by AID in the second and third categories above—that is, development advisers and development operators. At present, these two groups constitute the great majority of the Agency's professional specialists in non-administrative fields. In February 1962, of approximately 2,500 non-administrative specialists in the direct employ of the Agency's foreign service, more than 2,000 were considered to fall within these groups, as against fewer than 500 development planners and managers.* In addition, there were about 1,700 employees of contractors of AID, over 500 employees of other Federal agencies, and nearly 100 AID consultants working for AID on development projects overseas.

DEVELOPMENT POLICIES AND NEEDS FOR SPECIALIZED PERSONNEL

Recommendation 35

At the earliest possible date, AID should establish firm policies and objectives with respect to development assistance in each overseas country; and on this basis it should, insofar as practicable, develop estimates of present and future needs for specialized personnel in each subject-matter field.

Without firm understandings as to the development roles of the United States in different countries, it is impossible to determine what AID's needs for specialized personnel are or what they may become. In considering what these roles should be, the following questions need to be answered:

a. In any given country, to what extent should the United States assist the host government in *formulating* development programs and projects?

b. To what extent should the United States attempt to supply specialized personnel to (1) *advise* the host government on how approved projects should be launched and operated, (2) actually *operate* projects after they have been launched?

The President's Task Force on Foreign Assistance in 1961 believed that the initiative in formulating both programs and projects should, to the maximum practicable extent, come from the host government. It questioned the "balanced mission" concept, under which a set of specialists representing the relevant professional fields was considered essential for each AID mission abroad. It believed that project priorities must be established, that a pragmatic approach to development should be taken, and that the number of specialists needed in each field would vary with the agreed-upon development goals of the country.

The Committee understands that it is currently approved United States policy to facilitate the assumption by host governments of increasingly greater responsibility for both development planning and

---

* For a classification by types of specialists, see Chapter IV, p. 57.

development operations.* But the present capacities of these nations, both to plan and to carry out, are vastly unequal. It is desirable that, as rapidly as feasible, realistic development assistance policies covering the present and comparatively near future be formulated for each country.

These policies will provide a basis for estimating future needs for United States specialized technical assistance personnel in each subject-matter field, and will be useful in shaping recruitment efforts and in planning programs to increase the supply of development specialists in areas where current resources are inadequate.

QUALITATIVE NEEDS
Recommendation 36

AID should encourage educational institutions and professional societies which train and represent professionals in specialties involved in international development to build the field of development into the professions themselves; it should also encourage employers of professional personnel to make them available for overseas assignments without disadvantage to the individuals concerned or their careers.

The shortage of quality in regard to specialized personnel who could serve abroad is more acute than the shortage of quantity. Quality has at least two major elements: professional competence in the specialty concerned, and knowledge of how to apply this competence to development problems.

Professional competence is especially important in AID because the problems its specialized personnel are called upon to deal with are often more complex than those in their normal professional pursuits at home. Furthermore, host countries understandably resent, and often refuse to accept, persons proposed as advisers who are considered junior or undistinguished by their professional colleagues in the United States. Yet AID has found it difficult, in all the special-

---

*There will continue to be, in certain countries, a need for some personnel in the third category (development operators) for some time. Furthermore, it is now widely recognized that personnel at the middle level of professional development can be very useful in underdeveloped countries in operating capacities or as immediate assistants and aides to operators. The program of the Peace Corps, and the current expectation that a number of other countries will develop comparable programs, attest to this. The Committee recognizes the importance of such programs to provide "middle-level manpower," but offers no suggestions in this regard since they are beyond the terms of reference of its study.

116

ized fields, to attract established professionals. There are a number of reasons for this, among them the very real sense of isolation from their professions that specialized personnel get when sent abroad. Their normal career promotional patterns may also be adversely affected. Consequently, many of the most qualified professionals stay at home.

The second element, ability to apply professional competence to development problems, is even more crucial, and is more difficult to find and to predict. The problems of achieving development in foreign lands, through unfamiliar peoples and institutions or through new institutions that must be created for the purpose, are not within the normal range of education and experience of most professionals in the United States. We have many experts in education, but few in development education; many in public administration, but few in development administration; many in agriculture, but few in development agriculture.

The best way to mobilize our rich potential for overseas development work is to build the field of development into the professions themselves and into the institutions that train and represent these professions. A number of specific steps are possible, and all of them have already been instituted at one or another place or by one or another profession:

- the establishment, in professional schools, of courses and even major fields in the foreign development aspects of the profession;
- the establishment, on university campuses, of institutes or professorial chairs in foreign development;
- the encouragement, in graduate university courses, of major fields and of thesis studies of some aspect of foreign development;
- the establishment, within professional societies, of sections or committees devoted to the development aspects of the profession; and even the growth of societies within professional fields wholly devoted to foreign development;
- the encouragement, both on campuses and at other appropriate institutions, of research programs in aspects of foreign development.

Employers of professional personnel—whether they be universities, business, other agencies of the Federal Government, state or local governments, consulting firms, or labor unions—should be encouraged to make it possible, and even desirable, for their qualified people to take overseas assignments as development advisers without prejudice to—and preferably to the advantage of—their professional careers at home. Such steps should include the removal of impediments or "disincentives" such as threats to tenure, status, advancement, and retirement benefits for professional personnel taking overseas assignments.

DEVELOPMENT CAREERS FOR PROFESSIONAL SPECIALISTS

Recommendation 37

Except for the relatively small number necessary for planning and managing development programs, AID should not offer career status to professional specialists. But AID should encourage the recognition in each relevant specialty of foreign development as an important career pursuit, regardless of employer.

It has been suggested by some that large numbers of professional specialists be employed by AID on a career basis in order to build up continuity, experience, and dedication to the organization's objectives. The Committee believes that, with the exception of those responsible for planning and managing overseas programs, such a policy would be a mistake for several reasons. First, the requirements of AID's program preclude a permanent career service because the needs for specialized personnel abroad change each year. AID must keep flexible in its programing and operations. Second, better personnel will be obtained by hiring persons for temporary tours of duty. They will be forced to identify with their profession; those trying to escape from their professions will not be attracted. Third, the right professional opportunities for a permanent career service are missing in AID, at least so far as most specialized overseas personnel are concerned. The nature of the positions needed varies from time to time, and rotating such personnel from country to country satisfactorily is difficult.

But the decisive reason not to include these specialists in an AID career system is that, in the main, the career contexts and career loyalties of the best professionals lie with their professions and the whole range of activities with which those professions are associated. An association with AID, even if it could be made permanent, would not attract very many of the best professionals to spend most of their working lives overseas, far from their professional colleagues and the stimulus of professional association.

It should also be recognized that in most of these professional fields there are a variety of potential employers concerned with development, both at home and overseas. Given the mobility of professional personnel in the United States, an attractive career context usually involves relations with several different employers, not just one. And

118

AID can only benefit from the relevant experience specialized personnel may receive elsewhere.

This proposal that the bulk of AID specialist personnel not be hired on a career basis does not preclude the engagement of qualified individuals on two, three, or more different tours of duty, whether or not interrupted by other employment. In fact, repeat tours for qualified persons with development experience should be encouraged. Furthermore, some of them—experienced in, and dedicated to, development work—will qualify for career positions as development planners and managers. Such persons should be a major source of recruitment for the AID career service.

METHODS OF EMPLOYMENT

Recommendation 38

AID should have flexible procedures for engaging its temporary specialists, adapted in each case to the nature of the profession involved, the region and country of assignment, and the particular job to be done; but, in every case, merit and promise of effective performance should govern, and special protections should be provided against political and other pressures.

A number of means of engaging professional personnel are available to AID. These include: direct hire; agreements with other Federal agencies; and several kinds of contracts. In the opinion of the Committee, AID should retain wide flexibility in determining the best means of employing specialists for its different tasks in different countries. These depend to some extent on the nature, structure, and locus of the profession concerned. They depend also on the particular conditions of the country to which assignment is to be made. However the employment is arranged, its terms and duration should be made specific, either in relation to a terminal date or to the completion of a defined project.

But given such fluidity in the employment of professional specialists, whether hired directly or indirectly, and given the special vulnerability of AID to political and other pressures not necessarily related to fitness, it is most important for the Agency to satisfy itself that all individuals sent abroad are in fact professionally qualified in their fields. For assignments to be carried out by direct-hire specialists, standards should be developed to spell out the qualifications for effective performance. All candidates should be reviewed against these standards, and only those who fully measure up to them should be accepted. For development activities to be carried out through contractual arrangements, the Agency does not need to pass upon the technical qualifications of each individual engaged by the contractor. It must, however, give special attention to the quality and reliability of potential contractors, and, consistent with legal requirements, select only those who can be relied upon to attract and utilize the highly qualified individuals needed to achieve the objectives of the contract.

RECRUITMENT OF PROFESSIONAL SPECIALISTS
Recommendation 39

AID should institute an aggressive and continuing recruiting program designed to expand and to tap the most appropriate institutional resources in each professional field; its recruitment, like its method of employment, should be tailored to the particular nature of each professional field.

AID should use continuing and organized machinery for maintaining contacts with the leaders and institutions of each appropriate profession, and for obtaining their recommendations as to well-qualified individuals who might serve on temporary assignments. The organization and employment pattern of every profession is in some degree unique, and the recruiting effort for each should be geared to it. In some instances, another agency or bureau of the Federal Government is a principal employer of specialists in its field or has intimate acquaintance with the leaders in its professional field. The Committee believes that such Federal agencies have a special responsibility to make highly qualified specialists available to AID for temporary overseas assignments, without prejudice to their domestic careers. In other cases, the best sources are state and local governments, as in the instances of education, public safety, sanitation, and a number of specialized fields of public management. For industrial engineers, leaders in organization and management, specialists in sales, marketing, trade, and the like, the best sources are private businesses and commercial contractors. The universities and professional associations can be mobilized to provide leaders in various disciplines in the social and cultural sciences. It would be helpful, in this connection, if the appropriate professional associations were to establish machinery for continuing liaison with the agencies, including AID, that need technical specialists for overseas work.

Systematic efforts should be made by AID to tap these existing sources. In addition, AID should attempt to expand the base on which it can draw by stimulating an interest on the part of these and other potential sources in wider participation in the development assistance field.

TRAINING AND ORIENTATION
Recommendation 40

New professional personnel, prior to assignment overseas, should receive fundamental orientation with regard to AID, its mission, its organization, its administrative practices, and the region and country of assignment.

In the past, large numbers of professional specialists have been sent abroad with no orientation of any kind about the program in which they are to be engaged or about the conditions in the country for which they are destined. This is particularly true of the employees of AID contractors. In 1959-60, only four employees of contractors took the AID orientation course; in 1960-61, the number was seventeen. Yet there are about 1,700 contractual employees overseas.

Furthermore, employees of contractors as well as other non-career specialists of AID should be authorized and, where feasible, required to participate in the field orientation programs given at their post of assignment. Such employees should also participate in langauge instruction, both in Washington and at the post of assignment, when their facility in the local language is inadequate and when the duration of their service warrants such an investment.

A COURSE

OF ACTION

X

"The plain fact is that good policy demands both good men and good machinery. And though it may be true that good men can triumph over poor machinery, it is also true that they are more effective when they work with good machinery."

HENRY M. JACKSON

SUMMARY

The Department of State should spearhead interagency efforts to implement the Committee's proposals as soon as possible. These efforts should include:

- prompt submission of draft legislation to the Congress authorizing an Executive Under Secretary of State, a National Foreign Affairs College, and a foreign affairs personnel structure and system;
- early institution of administrative actions that can be taken under existing legislative authority and corollary strengthening of agency machinery and quality of staff engaged in important personnel activities;
- development of a coordinated, systematic program of personnel research.

THE COMMITTEE URGES that the proposals contained in this report be put into effect as soon as possible. Many of them require joint efforts by the three foreign affairs agencies, working closely with the

Civil Service Commission, the Bureau of the Budget, appropriate Congressional committees, and private organizations. The Department of State should take the leadership in respect to proposals that affect the interests of more than one agency.

The Committee suggests that the Secretary of State and the heads of the Agency for International Development and the United States Information Agency designate a high-level interagency committee to review its proposals, determine which require joint action, assign priorities, and oversee the activities of task forces established to work on specific aspects of the improvement program. This committee would be the forerunner of the proposed Board of Foreign Affairs Personnel, which should be formally constituted as soon as the new Executive Under Secretary has been appointed. The committee should report periodically to the Secretary of State and the other agency heads.

While the Committee anticipates that action on its proposals will be pursued vigorously, the task should be undertaken in an orderly manner and followed in the years ahead with as much consistency as changing circumstances permit. Hasty improvisation is no substitute for carefully conceived plans.

NEEDED LEGISLATION

Recommendation 41

Draft legislation authorizing the establishment of an office of Executive Under Secretary of State, and a second measure creating the proposed National Foreign Affairs College, should be submitted immediately to the Congress. These measures should be followed by submission of a comprehensive bill (to be known as the Foreign Affairs Personnel Act of 1963) authorizing the establishment of a foreign affairs personnel system.

The Committee attaches the highest importance to the early drafting of the legislation needed to implement its proposals. It suggests that the legislative program be undertaken in two stages, as follows:

Stage I would involve the immediate preparation of two separate legislative measures for consideration by the 1st Session of the 88th Congress: one to authorize the establishment of the proposed office of Executive Under Secretary of State (by appropriate amendment of Public Law 73, 81st Congress, as amended), and the second, a new bill, to create the proposed National Foreign Affairs College. These measures should be presented to the Congress in the context of the Committee's over-all proposals.

Early submission of legislation authorizing the establishment of a new post of Executive Under Secretary is vital in view of the importance the Committee attaches to this position.

A separate bill authorizing creation of a National Foreign Affairs College would recognize the urgency attached to this proposal as well as the special character of the proposed institution, the Government-wide scope of its mission, and its organizational location within the Executive Branch. Its provisions should be flexible enough to permit the evolution of education and training programs to meet a variety of needs and should permit recruitment of the highest-quality faculty and staff solely on the basis of interest in and capacity to promote the purposes of the College. Other provisions should: set forth the objectives of the proposed measure; indicate the composition and functions of the governing board; provide for the appointment and duties of the chancellor; define in general terms the various categories of persons to whom the facilities and programs of the institution may be made available; and provide the ground rules for financing. The legislation should authorize the new College to: contract for services; engage in research and evaluation activities; receive bequests and gifts; make grants and other forms of payment to co-operating institutions; and acquire real property. The new legislation should, by amendment of the Foreign Service Act of 1946, as amended, abolish the Foreign Service Institute.

Stage II of the legislative program would involve the early drafting of comprehensive legislation which should be referred to as the "Foreign Affairs Personnel Act of 1963." This measure would replace the Foreign Service Act of 1946, as amended, but would incorporate many of the provisions of that Act. It would provide the authority required to carry out the Committee's proposals relating to a family of compatible services encompassing the respective foreign services of the Department of State, USIA, and AID. Hence, it would authorize the establishment of career services for the conduct of foreign information and foreign assistance activities in accordance with the recommendations contained in Chapter III. This legislation should include provisions to bring the Civil Service employees of the three agencies within their respective foreign affairs systems, and authorize the agencies by administrative action to put this particular proposal into effect over a period of time.

It should be possible to ready the comprehensive legislative program for submission to the Congress by about mid-1963. The Committee suggests that the following points be kept in mind in drafting this legislation:

1. In general, authority to prescribe regulations might best be vested in the President (as it is with regard to the regulations governing

the Civil Service) and delegated by him in such a manner as will assure that the personnel systems are parallel and compatible. The Secretary of State could be delegated authority to review and approve regulations applicable to all three agencies.

2. The basic legislation should afford statutory safeguards to assure that the personnel process, including appointment, is protected from political and other adverse pressures.

3. Such basic subjects as personnel categories, compensation, appointment, commissioning, assignment, evaluation, promotion, retirement, and separation should be given appropriate legislative coverage in the new Act.

4. Each agency should be authorized to assign personnel for training at Government expense, to detail personnel to serve on the faculty or staff of the National Foreign Affairs College, and to conduct internal agency training programs as appropriate.

5. The legislation should contain whatever temporary provisions are needed to effect a just and orderly conversion of presently employed personnel to the new system.

ADMINISTRATIVE ACTION

Recommendation 42

Administrative improvements not requiring new legislative authority should be undertaken without delay. These include: the institution of programing systems, manpower planning, strengthened junior officer recruitment and development programs, the career-lines concept, and development and wider selection of career executives. Administrative machinery and staffs to carry out these improvements should be strengthened as necessary.

The Committee has not attempted to enumerate here the many administrative steps that can be taken under existing legislative authority to improve foreign affairs personnel management. Many of these steps are indicated in other chapters of this report; several, however, merit special emphasis:

1. Early institution of a programing system covering the range of foreign affairs activities, and of a manpower planning system that will provide meaningful projections of personnel needs.

2. Administrative actions designed to achieve closer affinity in personnel policies and operations among the Department of State, USIA, and AID, including joint recruitment efforts, increased interchange of personnel, and greater standardization of personnel

regulations, especially those affecting employee benefits.

3. Careful study of the mechanics for accommodating the Civil Service personnel of the three agencies within their respective foreign affairs personnel systems.

4. More flexible and positive recruitment of junior officers, more rapid promotion of junior officers up to class 5, the development in all the agencies of a supervised junior officer intern program, and a general tightening up of personnel standards, especially in the initial appointment of Reserve Officers and promotion of junior officers to class 5 and of mid-career officers to the senior levels.

5. Early implementation of the Committee's proposals concerning career lines and career stages that will adequately recognize the specialized aspects of foreign affairs work in relation to recruitment, examination, assignment, promotion, career development, and training.

6. Intensified efforts to spot executive talent and to provide appropriate developmental experience and professional training for those with executive ability; and institution of measures for the assessment of senior personnel of all three agencies leading to the development of a pool of top-quality executives for assignment to important posts across agency lines.

Implementation of the Committee's proposals calls for strengthening the existing administrative machinery and upgrading the caliber of officers assigned to important personnel functions. Strong and largely new staffs will be required for the development and installation of programing systems and manpower planning; the staffing for recruitment, selection, training, and career development activities should also be strengthened. For example, the Committee notes with concern the pathetically undernourished state of the career development program in the State Department.

PERSONNEL RESEARCH

Recommendation 43

Under the leadership of the Department of State, a coordinated interagency program of personnel research should be developed as a tool to guide continuing personnel improvements.

In the course of its explorations, the Committee became increasingly aware of the need for more systematic data and knowledge whereby current and past policies and practices in the personnel field might better be evaluated and new and improved ones might be developed.

Some of the more conspicuous gaps, such as that in the field of manpower requirements, have been noted elsewhere in this report. Ongoing research into a variety of problems, a few of which are suggested in the questions below, would appear very nearly indispensable to forward-looking personnel programs:

What are the fundamental elements of important classes of jobs at home and abroad, and what are the basic qualifications for them?

What kinds of people are attracted through existing methods of recruitment, and what kinds are missed? What are the main reasons, both for the positive and negative responses?

What kinds of persons—in terms of personality, intelligence, education—pass and fail written and oral entrance examinations?

How valid are the entrance examinations in terms of subsequent success or failure on the job?

To what extent do different kinds of training programs contribute to effectiveness on different kinds of jobs?

What are the kinds and frequency of emotional and nervous difficulties among overseas employees and their families? At what kinds of posts and countries do they most frequently occur, and among what types of persons and at what stages in their careers? To what extent can individuals susceptible to such difficulties be identified in advance and by what means?

Questions of these kinds could fruitfully be addressed to virtually every aspect of personnel administration from the determination of manpower requirements to retirement. And although research seldom, if ever, can provide specific and final answers, it can furnish invaluable guides and insights.

Present resources for personnel research are relatively slim. At the moment, for example, the personnel research staff of the Department of State consists of one full-time professional person. During the current year, AID has begun some research efforts along these lines, principally through contractual arrangements with private organizations. Many of the personnel problems of the foreign affairs agencies are similar, and this will be even more true when they are operating as a family of services. The Committee therefore believes that research efforts of these agencies need to be expanded and coordinated. Some projects should be carried on as merged or joint undertakings.

The military services and private business have long recognized the value of professional research in human relations and in personnel management. Such research efforts are at least as necessary in the foreign affairs services.

The improvement program proposed in this report is likely to call for moderate increases in funds, at least during the first year or so. The Committee believes that such additional funds as may be required are small in terms of the demands of the new diplomacy for men and women of the highest quality.

APPENDIX A

Concerning the Committee
on Foreign Affairs Personnel

I. TERMS OF REFERENCE FOR CONDUCT OF FOREIGN AFFAIRS PERSONNEL STUDY

One of the critical problems facing the United States in the 'Sixties is that of providing the necessary staff of the best qualified individuals for the conduct of American foreign relations in all its aspects. However good policies may be, they cannot be fully effective unless the quality of the individuals who must carry them out is of the highest order.

There is therefore an urgent need for a full dress study of the requirements now and in the foreseeable future for personnel to carry on the Foreign affairs of the United States, and of the principles and methods of selection, education and training, and career development that must be adopted and applied to meet those requirements.

AUSPICES

An inquiry into problems of selection, education and training and career development of foreign affairs personnel is being undertaken under the auspices of the Carnegie Endowment for International Peace.

PURPOSES

The purposes are to analyze and forecast as accurately as possible the United States Government's personnel requirements in the foreign affairs field over the next decade, and to strengthen the ability of the Government to find, develop, and make maximum use of personnel with the skills and talents required.

SCOPE

The inquiry will focus on the personnel needs of the Department of State, both foreign service and civil service, the United States Information Agency, the several aid agencies, and other agencies within the Department of State. While it will not deal directly with personnel requirements in the foreign affairs field of other agencies of the United States Government, it will of necessity give consideration to personnel problems having relevance to its central task.

The inquiry should evaluate and make recommendations on:

a) The recruitment of such personnel at the entrant level, including educational prerequisites, field recruitment and university liaison, and objectives and methods of testing, selection and career development prognosis.

b) The recruitment of such personnel at advanced levels, including the question of when it is desirable to recruit personnel by lateral entry, employ personnel for limited periods, or fill needs by career development from within.

c) Programs for career development, for the most efficient use of career personnel, and for the equalization of opportunities and the exchange of personnel among the several services.

d) Arrangements for in-career education and training at all levels. Attention should be paid to the relative values of education or training provided in the Foreign Service Institute, in other governmental training institutions, and in outside institutions. The efficiency of arrangements for the provision and training under these auspices should be evaluated, with particular reference to the organization and curriculum of the Foreign Service Institute.

e) The personnel administration of the Department of State and its relationship to those of the United States Information Agency, the several aid agencies, and other agencies within the Department.

RELATIONSHIP TO THE UNITED STATES GOVERNMENT

The study will be completely independent of Government influence or control. It will, however, receive the facilitating cooperation of the Department of State. There should be unrestricted access in this country and abroad to personnel under the authority of the Secretary of State and, to the extent necessary for the purposes of the inquiry, to personnel of other Government agencies. No government department or agency will be responsible in any way for the findings or recommendations of the study.

METHOD OF OPERATION

1. The survey is being undertaken by a committee of carefully selected, respected and experienced outstanding citizens, serviced

by a small staff headed by a competent senior director.

2. This pattern has been determined upon for the following reasons:
a) Clearly, a great deal of data collection and analysis will be needed, and this can be achieved only if there is a competent full-time working staff.

b) Since the survey is directed toward recommendations on a problem of national importance, it is desirable that they reflect the considered consensus of a small number of outstanding citizens who have had experience relevant to the problems of selection, education and training, and career development of foreign affairs personnel.
c) Moreover, since the survey will be pointed toward recommendations that can be implemented, in a setting in which there will be diverse interests at stake, some of them perhaps finding political reflection, it is desirable that the recommendations have the support of a group of respected individuals whose endorsement of the proposals may be expected to carry weight with the Administration, the Congress, and the general public.

3. The committee might be called "Committee on Foreign Affairs Personnel." It should be constituted as follows: Chairman—The Honorable Christian A. Herter; a former Foreign Service Officer; a former non-Foreign Service Ambassador or senior State Department official; individuals having high-level experience with respect to overseas information, overseas aid, civil service and public administration, and overseas business; an educator; a former member of the Wriston Committee; and Carnegie Endowment Trustees.

4. The committee should envisage conducting much of its work through working groups or task forces, each one of which should be chaired by a member of the committee and include as appropriate other members of the committee and/or other specially qualified individuals. Each working group should be given a carefully defined task, covering some part of the committee's total assignment as set forth under the heading of "Specific Tasks" above. There should not necessarily be a working task force for each of the subheadings in that section. In some cases there may be more than one task force covering a particular subheading. In other cases a task force might deal with parts of more than one subheading, and in still other cases the committee as a whole may want to address itself to a particular question.

5. The survey should be completed by the publication of a comprehensive report, but the committee should also seek as desirable and feasible to prepare interim reports which may or may not be made public, as the committee may determine.

II. MEMBERS OF THE COMMITTEE AND ITS STAFF

Members of the Committee

CHRISTIAN A. HERTER, *Chairman.* Former Secretary of State.

DON K. PRICE, *Vice-Chairman.* Dean of the Graduate School of Public Administration, Harvard University. Formerly: Vice President for International Activities, The Ford Foundation; Deputy Chairman, Research and Development Board, Department of Defense; Associate Director, Public Administration Clearing House.

GEORGE V. ALLEN, President, Tobacco Institute, Inc. Retired Foreign Service Officer. Formerly: Ambassador to Iran, Yugoslavia, India and Nepal, and Greece; Assistant Secretary of State; Director of the United States Information Agency.

KENNETH B. CLARK, Professor of Psychology, City College of New York; Special Adviser, Office of Personnel, Department of State; Research Director, Northside Center for Child Development.

CARLISLE H. HUMELSINE, President, Colonial Williamsburg, Inc. Formerly: Director of the Office of Departmental Administration, Department of State; Deputy Under Secretary of State for Administration; Assistant Secretary of State.

JOSEPH E. JOHNSON, President, Carnegie Endowment for International Peace. Formerly: State Department official and adviser to United States delegations at several international conferences.

MILTON KATZ, Director of International Legal Studies, Harvard Law School. Formerly: United States Special Representative in Europe, with rank of Ambassador; Chief of United States Delegation, Economic Commission for Europe; Chairman of Finance and Economic Committee of NATO.

JAMES A. PERKINS, Vice President, Carnegie Corporation of New York. Formerly: Assistant to Administrator, Foreign Economic Administration; Vice President of Swarthmore College; member of the Gaither Committee; consultant to the Department of Defense.

JAMES ROWE, Attorney. Formerly: Administrative Assistant to the President; Assistant Attorney General; public member, Foreign Service Selection Board, Department of State; member, First Hoover Commission; Chairman, Advisory Committee on Personnel to the Secretary of State.

JAMES HOPKINS SMITH, JR. Formerly: Director, International Cooperation Administration; Assistant Secretary of the Navy for Air.

ARTHUR K. WATSON, President, IBM World Trade Corporation.

JOHN HAY WHITNEY, Publisher of New York *Herald Tribune*. Formerly: Ambassador to Great Britain; special adviser and consultant on public affairs, Department of State; member, Commission on Foreign Economic Policy; member, Secretary of State's Public Committee on Personnel.

The Committee Staff

FREDERICK C. MOSHER, *Staff Director*. Professor of Political Science, the University of California, Berkeley. Formerly: professor at Syracuse University and the University of Bologna, Italy; officer in the Department of State, UNRRA, War Department.

ARTHUR G. JONES, *Associate Staff Director*. Foreign Service Officer. Recently: Counselor for Administration, U.S. Embassy, New Delhi; Formerly: personnel officer, TVA; on staff of Rowe Committee and White House Personnel Task Force.

GERALD W. BUSH. Formerly: teaching and research assistant, Department of Political Science, the University of California, Berkeley.

BARRY CASPER, Personnel Officer, AID. Formerly: economic analyst for Department of Commerce; personnel officer, TVA and AEC.

FRANCES FIELDER, Personnel Management Specialist, Department of the Navy. Formerly: on staff of Survey Research Center, Michigan State University; personnel experience with Federal agencies.

JOHN E. HARR. Formerly: United Press reporter; Information Officer for USIA in Tel Aviv, Israel; in charge of communications programs at University College, The University of Chicago, and University Extension, the University of California, Berkeley.

ROENE B. HORGAN. Formerly: Foreign Service Officer; personnel officer in the Department of State.

FORDYCE W. LUIKART, Senior staff member, The Brookings Institution. Formerly: with Civil Service Commission; Department of Health, Education, and Welfare; Federal Aviation Agency; First Hoover Commission; Task Force on Training and Orientation for AID.

NATHAN MACCOBY, Professor of Mass Communications, Stanford University. Formerly: in Government personnel work and participant in attitude studies in the Army psychological group.

R. KENNETH OAKLEY, Foreign Service Officer. Recently: Chief, Intelligence Collection and Distribution, Department of State.

EVERETT W. REIMER, Social Development Adviser, the Alliance for Progress, AID. Formerly: Director of Personnel for OPA; staff member, Second Hoover Commission; Secretary of the Comittee on Human Resources of the Commonwealth of Puerto Rico.

III. LETTER OF INVITATION TO COMMITTEE MEMBERS FROM MR. JOSEPH E. JOHNSON

22 August 1961

Dear ⎯⎯⎯⎯⎯:

The Carnegie Endowment for International Peace, on the initiative of the Department of State, is undertaking a survey of personnel requirements of the United States Government in the foreign affairs field. The survey is described in the attached memorandum, "The Selection, Education and Training and Career Development of Foreign Affairs Personnel: Proposed Survey to be undertaken under the auspices of the Carnegie Endowment for International Peace."

Secretary of State Dean Rusk has given the proposed survey his enthusiastic endorsement, and has expressed his belief that it will be "in the national interest."

The survey will be conducted by a committee of respected and outstanding citizens. I am pleased to be able to tell you that the Hon. Christian A. Herter has agreed to serve as Chairman of the committee.

There will be a small staff under the direction of Professor Frederick C. Mosher of the University of California at Berkeley.

On behalf of Mr. Herter, and of the Carnegie Endowment, I have the honor of asking you to serve as a member of the survey committee. The Carnegie Endowment has accepted responsibility for this survey after a careful investigation of the contribution it might be expected to make to the important goal of strengthening the quality and administration of United States foreign affairs personnel in the crucial years ahead. I have concluded that such a survey is both necessary and timely and that the one proposed may indeed make a strategic contribution on this crucial problem. I hope very much therefore—and I speak for Mr. Herter as well—that we may look forward to your cooperation in this enterprise. . . .

Sincerely yours,

/s/

Joseph E. Johnson

Enclosure

IV. LETTER TO COMMITTEE MEMBERS FROM THE HONORABLE DEAN RUSK

August 24, 1961

Dear _____:

I hope you will find it possible to accept the invitation you have received from Joseph E. Johnson, President of Carnegie Endowment for International Peace, to serve under the chairmanship of the Honorable Christian A. Herter as a member of a committee to conduct a survey on "the selection, education and training, and career development of foreign affairs personnel."

I regard that survey as having great potential importance on a matter which is not only one of my central concerns but can also fairly be described as highly relevant to the national interest. I can assure you that the Department of State will give its fullest support to the survey.

Sincerely yours,

/s/

Dean Rusk

V. INDIVIDUALS WHO APPEARED BEFORE THE FULL COMMITTEE ON FOREIGN AFFAIRS PERSONNEL *

David E. Bell, Director, Bureau of the Budget.

Charles E. Bohlen, Special Assistant to the Secretary of State.

Mrs. Charles E. Bohlen, Vice President, Association of American Foreign Service Women.

McGeorge Bundy, Special Assistant to the President.

Mrs. James M. Byrne, President, Association of American Foreign Service Women.

Harlan Cleveland, Assistant Secretary of State for International Organization Affairs.

William J. Crockett, Assistant Secretary of State for Administration.

Allen W. Dulles (former Director, Central Intelligence Agency).

Ralph A. Dungan, Special Assistant to the President.

Dennis A. FitzGerald, Consultant, Agency for International Development (and former Deputy Director for Operations, International Cooperation Administration).

Fowler Hamilton, Administrator, Agency for International Development.

Loy W. Henderson (former Deputy Under Secretary of State for Administration).

Roger W. Jones, Deputy Under Secretary of State for Administration.

John W. Macy, Jr., Chairman, U.S. Civil Service Commission.

William H. Orrick, Jr., Deputy Under Secretary of State for Administration.

Herman Pollack, Deputy Assistant Secretary of State for Personnel.

William H. Weathersby, Director of Personnel, United States Information Agency.

Donald M. Wilson, Deputy Director, United States Information Agency.

---

* Showing positions held at the time of appearance.

VI. OVERSEAS POSTS VISITED BY COMMITTEE MEMBERS AND STAFF

LATIN AMERICA: Argentina—*Buenos Aires*
Bolivia—*La Paz*
Chile—*Santiago*
Colombia—*Bogota*
Jamaica—*Kingston*
Peru—*Lima*
Trinidad—*Port-of-Spain*
Venezuela—*Caracas*
Barbados

EUROPE: Belgium—*Brussels*
England—*London*
France—*Paris*, Special Mission USRO
Netherlands—*The Hague, Rotterdam*
USSR—*Moscow*

AFRICA: Ghana—*Accra*
Libya—*Tripoli*
Nigeria—*Ibadan, Lagos*
Senegal—*Dakar*
Sudan—*Khartoum*

FAR EAST: Hong Kong
Japan—*Tokyo, Yokohama*
Laos—*Vientiane*
Thailand—*Bangkok*

NEAR EAST AND SOUTH ASIA: Greece—*Athens*
Lebanon—*Beirut*
Pakistan—*Karachi*
Turkey—*Ankara, Istanbul*

.. In addition, several members of the Committee visited other posts on different missions and discussed some aspects of the Committee's work with selected officers.

VII. STUDIES MADE BY CONSULTANTS FOR THE COMMITTEE

The studies referred to below were prepared as working papers for the Committee's use and are not available for distribution. Some of them, together with other studies prepared by the Committee's staff, will be published in the near future.

1. BERTHA W. BEATON, Former Department of State Personnel Officer. Studies of certain aspects of the Foreign Service performance evaluation program and selection-out system.
2. ROBERT E. ELDER, Professor of Political Science, Colgate University. Studies of existing personnel arrangements of certain domestic agencies of the Government operating overseas, and of their relationship with the Foreign Service, as well as possible alternatives to these arrangements and relationships.
3. DOUGLAS V. LEPAN, Professor, Queen's University, Kingston, Ontario; retired member of the Canadian Diplomatic Service. A report on the organization and personnel management of the Canadian Diplomatic Service.
4. ARTHUR W. MACMAHON, Professor Emeritus, Columbia University. A perspective essay on problems and approaches to education and training for foreign affairs, and other studies.
5. WILLIAM P. MADDOX, Retired Foreign Service Officer; presently, Deputy Chairman of Advisory Staff, U.S. Arms Control and Disarmament Agency. Former Director, Foreign Service Institute.
   A report on the results of interviews with faculty and students at selected colleges and universities relating to recruitment for foreign affairs careers and educational programs and opportunities for post-entry training in foreign affairs.
6. THE NATIONAL OPINION RESEARCH CENTER, UNIVERSITY OF CHICAGO. Reports on career plans of June 1961 college graduates.
7. WALLACE S. SAYRE, Eaton Professor of Public Administration, Columbia University. A comparative analysis of the British and United States Foreign Services, and other studies.
8. ARTHUR G. STEVENS, Vice President, Mt. Sterling National Bank, Mt. Sterling, Kentucky; former Director of Personnel, International Cooperation Administration. A report on the basic framework of the Civil Service and Foreign Service personnel systemʳ and their relationship.
9. EDWARD W. WEIDNER, Vice Chancellor, East-West Center, University of Hawaii. A report on recruitment and selection of specialized personnel for United States technical assistance programs abroad with proposals for the future.

APPENDIX B

*Concerning Foreign
Affairs Personnel*

I. Summary of Legislative Background Relating to Foreign Affairs Personnel

Many different statutes govern personnel management in the several foreign affairs agencies. This legislation may be grouped, however, under several principal headings, as follows:

1. *Legislation Generally Applicable to Government Departments and Agencies*

   Certain legislation applies generally to the civilian employees of Government departments and agencies, including the foreign affairs agencies. Examples are legislation pertaining to leave benefits, health and group life insurance, premium pay, overseas allowances, transfers to international organizations, compensation of top executive officials, veterans' preference, political activities, conflict of interest, and incentive awards.

2. *Civil Service Legislation*

   Most of the departmental or headquarters personnel of the foreign affairs agencies are administered within the general Civil Service system, which in turn is based on a variety of statutes and executive orders, as well as regulations promulgated by the Civil Service Commission. Provisions relating to appointment, training, compensation, classification, promotions and performance rating, separation, and retirement, as examples, come within the purview of the various Civil Service laws and rules.

3. *The Foreign Service Act of 1946, as amended*

   Except for those statutes which apply generally to civilian employees of the Government, mentioned under 1 above, Foreign Service personnel of the Department of State are administered largely under the provisions of the Foreign Service Act of 1946, as amended, and regulations prescribed by the President and the Secretary of State pursuant

141

thereto. While the Foreign Service Act lays down basic prescriptions, it also vests considerable authority and discretion in the Secretary of State. In particular, it reflects the concept of rank-in-man. This Act also prescribes the various categories of personnel and the terms and conditions of their service in each instance, and covers all the subjects cited above in connection with Civil Service legislation.

Pursuant to Reorganization Plan No. 8, of June 1, 1953, as amended, and executive orders relating thereto, the foreign service employees of the United States Information Agency are administered within the provisions of the Foreign Service Act of 1946 relative to Foreign Service Reserve, Foreign Service Staff, and local or foreign national employees. Authorities vested in the Secretary of State are, with few exceptions, conferred on the Director of USIA. The Agency, however, is not authorized to employ Foreign Service Officers or to utilize authorities or provisions relating to Foreign Service Officers, such as selection-out and retirement.

The foreign service personnel of the Agency for International Development are administered within the framework of the Foreign Assistance Act of 1961, as amended. This Act makes available personnel authorities and provisions of the Foreign Service Act of 1946, as amended, relating to Foreign Service Reserve, Staff, and local employees. These authorities are supplemented by a number of special provisions pertaining to AID, including selection-out authority, authority to construct and utilize schools and hospitals for the use of United States personnel and their dependents abroad and several other special provisions of law.

It may be noted that both USIA and AID lack legally established career foreign services in the same sense as the Department of State proper.

II. Brief Summary of Previous Studies on Foreign Affairs Personnel

The Committee has taken into account in its own study a number of previous personnel studies, most of which dealt with the Department of State and its Foreign Service. The Committee was impressed by the fact that many of the basic conclusions and recommendations of these earlier reports, though formulated by different groups, and at different times, are essentially similar, and, further, coincide with many of the Committee's own proposals.

1. *Bureau of the Budget Proposals: August 1945* (Unpublished). A report to Secretary Byrnes by the Bureau of the Budget recommending organizational and personnel improvements in the Department and Foreign Service.

The report called for more modern and progressive personnel practices and elimination of barriers preventing effective recruitment and utilization of personnel. It proposed: substantial use of lateral entry appointments to the career Foreign Service; generally uniform classification and pay provisions as between the Civil Service and Foreign Service to facilitate transfer between the two services; more frequent and varied assignments of Foreign Service personnel to the Department and other Government agencies; greater emphasis on leadership and administrative skill in staffing supervisory posts; and establishment of a comprehensive in-service training program.

2. *The Chapin-Foster Report: October 1945* (Unpublished). A report principally by Mr. Seldon Chapin and Mr. Andrew Foster, both Foreign Service Officers, outlining a plan for the consolidation of Foreign Service and certain departmental personnel. (It was later decided to proceed with draft legislation limited to improvements in the Foreign Service itself. These legislative proposals subsequently became the Foreign Service Act of 1946.)

The consolidation plan envisaged a gradual merging of the Foreign Service and certain areas of the Department. The members of the consolidated service would be obligated to serve at home and abroad and would constitute an Executive Branch of general officers and a Staff Branch of specialists and support personnel. Assignment of these personnel would be flexible, some serving most of their careers in Washington and others primarily overseas. Persons employed only for duty in Washington would constitute a Departmental Branch.

3. *Report of the Commission on Organization of the Executive Branch of the Government: February 1949 (The First Hoover Commission).* A report dealing with the entire machinery of the Government for the conduct of foreign affairs but with particular reference to the organization and administration of the State Department and the Foreign Service.

The Commission's principal personnel recommendation relevant to the current study was that:

"The personnel in the permanent State Department establishment in Washington and the personnel of the Foreign Service above certain levels should be amalgamated over a short period of years into a single foreign affairs service obligated to serve at home or overseas, and constituting a safeguarded career group administered separately from the general Civil Service."

Professional personnel in the new service would be grouped into General officer and Special officer categories supplemented by a Staff category and a Reserve category, the latter to be used particularly to meet the overseas needs of other agencies of the Government. The report emphasized the need for more flexible recruitment and promotion policies in order to obtain and retain persons with special skills as well as general aptitudes.

4. *Report of the Secretary's Advisory Committee on Personnel: August 1950 (The Rowe Committee).* A report to Secretary Acheson recommending an improved personnel system for the conduct of foreign affairs.

The Committee's principal recommendation was that:

"There should be a single personnel system applicable to all people under the direct administrative control of the Secretary of State. Such a system would provide a unified, flexible group recruited and administered under a common set of policies. Employees would be assigned at home and abroad as the needs of the service might require. The requirement of serving at home and abroad, as a condition of employment, should be applied to those positions and organizational areas where it is necessary for satisfactory performance of duties. Because of the distinctive characteristics of the conduct of foreign affairs and the fact that many of the people concerned serve abroad, the system should be established initially outside of the regular Civil Service. This recommendation is made without prejudice to the possibility of eventual development and improvement of the Civil Service system that might result in making it suitable for all civilian employees of the Government. The integrated personnel system must take into account the interests of other Federal agencies concerned with foreign affairs."

The Committee recommended further: a positive program for the recruitment of the best available people for all levels subject to rigorous examination; development of career personnel to meet needs for executives, generalists, and specialists through a progressive system of training, placement, and promotion; increased assignments of personnel to other agencies; longer tours of duty at particular posts; career lines of advancement for specialists; and modification of selection-out in order to retain competent people at the middle grades. The new Foreign Affairs Service would include a Foreign Affairs Officer group and a Clerical-Technical group with provision for making both permanent and temporary appointments to each group. All personnel would be under a single salary schedule.

5. *The Brookings Institution Report: June 1951.* A comprehensive report by The Brookings Institution entitled *The Administration of Foreign Affairs and Overseas Operations* prepared for the Bureau of the Budget.

The personnel aspects of this report generally endorsed the previous proposals of the Hoover Commission and the Rowe Committee and emphasized the need for mobility and interchangeability in staffs, adequate specialization and training of personnel, pre-indoctrination for overseas service, greater decentralization of personnel authority, all within the framework of a foreign affairs personnel system inclusive of all, or nearly all, civilian foreign affairs staffs at home and abroad.

6. *Report of the Secretary's Public Committee on Personnel: May 1954 (The Wriston Committee).* A report to Secretary Dulles, later published under the title *Toward A Stronger Foreign Service,* proposing a number of measures to strengthen the effectiveness of the professional services under the Secretary of State.

The Committee's principal recommendation called for a partial but substantial integration of professional personnel in the Civil Service and the Foreign Service through a liberalized lateral entry process. The expanded Foreign Service Officer group would in future staff most professional positions at home and abroad, and the departmental Civil Service and Foreign Service staff groups would be contracted accordingly.

It proposed a more positive and expanded recruitment program, revised examination procedures, and a Foreign Service Scholarship Training Program leading to bottom-level appointments of Foreign Service Officers. The Committee urged a revitalization and strengthening of in-service training; development of long-term projections of personnel requirements and better utilization of people; more adequate recognition of specialization; improved monetary incentives; and measures designed to improve morale and public confidence.

7. *Report of the White House Foreign Affairs Personnel Task Force: 1954* (Unpublished). A report prepared by an interagency group of Government officials designed to lay the groundwork for more satisfactory personnel arrangements in the field of foreign affairs.

The report generally endorsed the proposals of the Rowe Committee, with extension of the framework of a foreign affairs personnel system initially to the State Department, USIA, and the Foreign Operations Administration.

The proposed system would be administered outside the general Civil Service. While each agency would have authority over its people, broad policy would be determined by the Executive Office of the President. The Task Force made a number of other recommendations relating to various phases of personnel administration.

8. *The Brookings Institution Report: November 1959.* A report prepared by The Brookings Institution, entitled *The Formulation and Administration of United States Foreign Policy,* for the Senate Committee on Foreign Relations.

The personnel aspects of this report were predicated upon the establishment of a new Department of Foreign Affairs that would encompass the activities of the Department of State, foreign aid activities, and foreign information programs. Many of the proposals advocated in earlier reports relating to the State Department and the Foreign Service were endorsed in this report, including the concept of career ladders for various occupational specialties, development of executive talent, inventory of personnel needs, increased lateral entry into the Foreign Service, a merit scholarship training program, and more adequate in-service training and career management.

III. Salary Comparison Table (Civil Service and Foreign Service)

The salary rates shown below were authorized by Public Law 87-793, 87th Congress. Rates shown under Phase I were effective October 14, 1962. Those shown under Phase II are to take effect on January 5, 1964. It is expected that additional legislation will be considered to increase further existing salary rates for grades GS-16, FSO-2 and FSR-2, and above.

Civil Service employees in the main are compensated under the General Schedule, which consists of 18 salary grades and is referred to in this chart as GS.

Category and Grade or Class			Salary Range	
GS	FSO–FSR	FSS	Phase I	Phase II
18	CA* —		$20,000	no change
	CM** —		19,800	no change
		1	18,975–19,650	no change
17			18,000–20,000	no change
16			16,000–18,000	no change
		2	15,900–18,900	no change
15			14,565–17,925	$15,665–19,270
		1	13,440–17,000	14,265–18,025
	3		13,440–16,110	14,265–17,085
14			12,845–16,245	13,615–17,215
13		2	11,150–14,070	11,725–14,805
	4		11,150–13,340	11,725–14,035
12			9,475–11,995	9,980–12,620
		3	9,315–11,755	9,695–12,255
	5		9,315–11,145	9,695–11,615
11			8,045–10,165	8,410–10,650
		4	7,705– 9,745	8,090–10,210
	6		7,705– 9,235	8,090– 9,680
10			7,290– 9,495	7,690– 9,985
		5	6,910– 8,980	7,295– 9,455
9			6,675– 8,700	7,030– 9,100
	7		6,475– 7,765	6,810– 8,160
		6	6,225– 8,115	6,570– 8,505
8			6,090– 7,935	6,390– 8,280
		7	5,610– 7,320	5,809– 7,645
7			5,540– 7,205	5,795– 7,550
	8		5,540– 6,650	5,795– 6,965
		8	5,060– 6,590	5,270– 6,845
6			5,035– 6,565	5,235– 6,810
		9	4,575– 5,930	4,715– 6,110
5			4,565– 6,005	4,690– 6,130
		10	4,110– 5,445	4,215– 5,525
4			4,110– 5,370	4,215– 5,475
3			3,820– 4,830	3,880– 4,900
2			3,560– 4,505	3,620– 4,565
1			3,245– 4,190	3,305– 4,250

* Career Ambassador.
** Career Minister.

146

IV. Statistics on Personnel in Foreign Affairs

1. General Personnel Strength

As shown by Table I, the Department of State employed as of June 30, 1962, 23,696 full-time employees composed of 13,733 United States citizens and 9,963 foreign national employees. United States personnel included 8,698 Foreign Service and 5,035 domestic or Civil Service employees. The Foreign Service group serves predominantly overseas, 6,685 being so assigned. However, a significant number, some 2,013, were assigned to the United States. The domestic or Civil Service group, on the other hand, is a home-based staff, concentrated primarily in Washington.

2. Categories of United States Foreign Service Personnel

United States foreign service personnel are divided into four categories, namely Chiefs of Mission, Foreign Service Officers, Foreign Service Reserve Officers, and Foreign Service Staff personnel. Personnel strength data for these categories are shown in Tables II, III, and IV.

a. Chiefs of Mission

Of the 96 Chiefs of Mission, 61, or about 64 per cent, were Foreign Service Officers, 5 with the rank of Career Ambassador, 28 in the class of Career Minister, and 28 Foreign Service Officers of class 1. The remaining 35 Chiefs of Mission were non-career appointees.

b. Foreign Service Officers

Excluding Foreign Service Officers serving as Chiefs of Mission, the FSO Corps numbered 3,626 officers, 2,374 of whom were assigned overseas. The remaining 1,252 were serving in the United States.

c. Foreign Service Reserve Officers

The Foreign Service Reserve Officer category included 1,235 officers, 847 of whom were assigned overseas and 388 to the United States.

d. Foreign Service Staff

The Foreign Service Staff category numbering 3,741 employees is a predominantly overseas group. Some 3,369 were serving abroad and only 372 were assigned to the United States.

TABLE I

DEPARTMENT OF STATE
Full-Time Employment

June 30, 1962

	All Areas		United States		Overseas	
	No.	%	No.	%	No.	%
Foreign Service Employees	8,698	36.7	2,013	28.6	6,685	40.2
Civil Service Employees	5,035	21.3	5,035	71.4	–	–
Total United States Citizen Employment	13,733	58.0	7,048	–	6,685	40.2
Foreign National Employees	9,963	42.0	–	–	9,963	59.8
Total Employment	23,696	100.0	7,048	100.0	16,648	100.0

TABLE II

DEPARTMENT OF STATE
Categories of United States Foreign Service Employees

June 30, 1962

	Total		United States		Overseas	
	No.	%	No.	%	No.	%
Chiefs of Mission	96	1.1	1	–	95	1.4
Non-career	(35)		(1)		(34)	
Foreign Service Officers	(61)				(61)	
Foreign Service Officers*	3,626	41.7	1,252	62.2	2,374	35.6
Foreign Service Reserve Officers	1,235	14.2	388	19.3	847	12.6
Foreign Service Staff Personnel	3,741	43.0	372	18.5	3,369	50.4
Total	8,698	100.0	2,013	100.0	6,685	100.0

* Excludes Foreign Service Officers serving as Chiefs of Mission.

148

TABLE III

DEPARTMENT OF STATE
Distribution of Foreign Service Officers and
Foreign Service Reserve Officers by Class

June 30, 1962

Class	FSO Number	FSO %	FSR Number	FSR %
Career Ambassador	7	0.2	—	—
Career Minister	48	1.3	—	—
1	223	6.0	60	4.8
2	407	11.0	91	7.4
3	607	16.5	184	14.9
4	721	19.5	243	19.7
5	572	15.5	286	23.2
6	323	8.8	189	15.3
7	382	10.4	126	10.2
8	397	10.8	56	4.5
Total	3,687	100.0	1,235	100.0

TABLE IV

DEPARTMENT OF STATE
Distribution of Foreign Service Staff Personnel by Class

June 30, 1962*

Class	Number	%
FSS–1	18	0.5
FSS–2	12	0.3
FSS–3	20	0.5
FSS–4	22	0.6
FSS–5	25	0.7
FSS–6	26	0.7
FSS–7	71	1.9
FSS–8	165	4.4
FSS–9	358	9.6
FSS–10	750	20.0
FSS–11	1,155	30.9
FSS–12	758	20.3
FSS–13	361	9.6
Total	3,741	100.0

* The several classes of FSS personnel were consolidated into ten classes, effective October 14, 1962.

3. Categories of Departmental Personnel

Departmental employees are mainly concentrated under the General Schedule grades of the Civil Service Classification Act. Substantially fewer are included under what is referred to as the Excepted Schedule—that is, the Secretary has authority to fix salaries for certain positions excepted from the regular Civil Service pay scale. In actuality, the same rates of compensation are applied to this group as apply to those under the General Schedule.

A third category is that known as Wage Board employees. Their pay is fixed on the basis of prevailing rates for comparable work. Examples are people engaged in offset printing or lithographic work.

Finally, there are the so-called Unclassified posts which are prescribed by statute, such as the Assistant Secretaries.

TABLE V

DEPARTMENT OF STATE
Distribution of Departmental Employees by Grade

*June 30, 1962 ***

Grade	Number	%
18	6	0.1
17	13	0.3
16	35	0.8
15	147	3.5
14	162	3.9
13	233	5.6
12	249	5.9
11	295	7.0
10	17	0.4
9	365	8.7
8	103	2.5
7	491	11.7
6	332	7.9
5	650	15.5
4	558	13.3
3	477	11.4
2	47	1.1
1	16	0.4
Total	4,196	100.0

* Not included in the above figures are (1) Wage Board employees, (2) officials serving in Unclassified posts, such as Assistant Secretaries, (3) employees assigned to the United States Mission to the United Nations in New York City, (4) employees of the International Boundary and Water Commissions, (5) contract employees, and (6) Excepted Schedule employees.

4. Functional Analysis of Foreign Service Officers

Table VI below shows a distribution by class of Foreign Service Officers in terms of their functional assignments or specialty in June 1962.

TABLE VI

DEPARTMENT OF STATE
Functional Distribution of Foreign Service Officers by Class

Present Specialty	CA	CM	0–1	0–2	0–3	0–4	0–5	0–6	0–7	0–8	Total	%	% in Specialty above 0–4
Political	1	2	32	106	177	178	85	50	28	11	670	18.3	47.5
Economic	–	1	14	70	128	126	72	40	47	13	511	13.9	41.7
Administrative	–	1	10	38	96	160	141	67	57	26	596	16.2	24.3
Consular	–	—	5	16	28	79	136	75	129	112	580	15.8	8.4
Program Direction	5	40	139	107	64	31	14	2	—	—	402	11.0	88.3
Commercial	–	—	1	9	25	43	35	9	7	2	131	3.6	26.7
Labor	–	—	—	8	7	9	5	1	—	—	30	0.8	50.0
International Organization	–	—	3	10	16	9	7	2	—	—	47	1.3	61.7
Intelligence and Research	–	—	4	9	10	26	12	4	1	8	74	2.0	31.1
Public Affairs	–	—	2	3	4	5	5	1	2	2	24	0.7	37.5
Cultural Affairs	–	—	—	6	3	8	11	3	6	12	49	1.3	18.4
Miscellaneous*	–	—	1	3	3	2	2	3	9	4	27	0.7	25.9
Not given**	1	4	9	19	42	42	47	66	93	206	529	14.4	—
Total	7	48	220	404	603	718	572	323	379	396	3,670	100.0	

* Includes Legal, Science, Geography, and Field Post operations.
** Includes officers in transit, training, over-complement at posts, leave status, etc.

B. UNITED STATES INFORMATION AGENCY

1. General Personnel Strength

As shown by Table VII below, the United States Information Agency employed as of June 30, 1962, 10,898 full-time employees composed of 4,191 United States citizens and 6,707 foreign national employees. United States personnel included 1,623 Foreign Service and 2,568 domestic or Civil Service employees. The Foreign Service group serves predominantly overseas, 1,330 being so assigned in contrast to 293 on assignment to the United States. The Civil Service group is a home-based staff, concentrated primarily in Washington.

TABLE VII

UNITED STATES INFORMATION AGENCY
Full-Time Employment
June 30, 1962 *

	All Areas		United States		Overseas	
	No.	%	No.	%	No.	%
Foreign Service Employees	1,623	14.9	293	10.3	1,330	16.5
Civil Service Employees	2,568	23.6	2,556	89.7	12	0.2
Total United States Citizen Employment	4,191	38.5	2,849	100.0	1,342	16.7
Foreign National Employees	6,707	61.5	–	–	6,707	83.3
Total Employment	10,898	100.0	2,849	100.0	8,049	100.0

* Excludes 39 employees on reimbursable detail to other agencies. Includes 4 Foreign Service Officers assigned to USIA.

2. Categories of United States Foreign Service Personnel

Foreign Service personnel of the Agency are divided into three categories, namely, Foreign Service Career Reserve Officers, Foreign Service Limited Reserve Officers, and Foreign Service Staff personnel. USIA lacks authority to itself employ Foreign Service Officers. Personnel strength data for these categories are shown in Tables VIII, IX, and X.

TABLE VIII

UNITED STATES INFORMATION AGENCY
Categories of United States Foreign Service Employees
June 30, 1962 *

	Total		United States		Overseas	
	No.	%	No.	%	No.	%
Foreign Service Career Reserve Officers	772	47.7	138	47.1	634	47.8
Foreign Service Limited Reserve Officers	267	16.5	35	11.9	232	17.5
Foreign Service Staff Personnel	580	35.8	120	41.0	460	34.7
Total	1,619	100.0	293	100.0	1,326	100.0

* Excludes 27 Career Reserve Officers and 12 Staff employees on reimbursable detail to other agencies, and also excludes 4 Foreign Service Officers assigned to USIA.

TABLE IX

UNITED STATES INFORMATION AGENCY
Distribution of Foreign Service Reserve Officers by Class
June 30, 1962

	Total		Career Reserve		Limited Reserve	
	No.	%	No.	%	No.	%
FSR–1	38	3.5	29	3.6	9	3.4
FSR–2	96	9.0	73	9.1	23	8.6
FSR–3	215	20.2	169	21.2	46	17.2
FSR–4	260	24.4	193	24.2	67	25.1
FSR–5	261	24.5	171	21.4	90	33.7
FSR–6	85	8.0	57	7.1	28	10.5
FSR–7	47	4.4	44	5.5	3	1.1
FSR–8	64	6.0	63	7.9	1	0.4
Total	1,066	100.0	799	100.0	267	100.0

TABLE X

UNITED STATES INFORMATION AGENCY
Distribution of Foreign Service Staff Personnel by Class
June 30, 1962

Class	Number	%
FSS–1	32	5.4
FSS–2	41	6.9
FSS–3	60	10.1
FSS–4	64	10.8
FSS–5	94	15.9
FSS–6	49	8.3
FSS–7	39	6.6
FSS–8	21	3.6
FSS–9	8	1.4
FSS–10	44	7.4
FSS–11	63	10.6
FSS–12	65	11.0
FSS–13	12	2.0
Total	592	100.0

3. Categories of Civil Service Personnel

Most headquarters employees are under the Civil Service personnel system and are mainly under the General Schedule grades of the Civil Service Classification Act.

TABLE XI

UNITED STATES INFORMATION AGENCY
Distribution of Civil Service Personnel by Grade
*June 30, 1962 ***

Grade	Number	%
18	3	0.1
17	7	0.3
16	11	0.5
15	66	2.8
14	152	6.5
13	248	10.6
12	286	12.2
11	289	12.4
10	61	2.6
9	229	9.8
8	21	0.9
7	201	8.6
6	89	3.8
5	308	13.2
4	224	9.6
3	124	5.3
2	18	0.8
1	1	–
Total	**2,338**	**100.0**

* Includes all GS and ES full-time personnel. Excludes 226 Wage Board personnel, 2 in Unclassified positions and 2 Presidential appointees.

4. Functional Distribution of USIA United States Citizen Personnel

Table XII below shows a distribution of USIA employees in the headquarters and overseas services. These data are as of June 30, 1961, but are generally indicative of current occupational groupings of the Agency's employees.

TABLE XII

UNITED STATES INFORMATION AGENCY
Functional Distribution of Personnel

June 30, 1961

HEADQUARTERS SERVICE*

	Number	% of Headquarters Service
Policy and Program Planning Advisers	148	5.5
Administration and Staff Personnel	469	17.6
Radio, TV, and Motion Picture Producers	131	4.9
Clerical and Crafts	726	27.2
Language Specialists	113	4.2
Graphic Arts Specialists	35	1.3
Writers and Editors	765	28.6
Librarians	39	1.5
Engineers and Equipment Technicians	246	9.2
Total	2,672	100.0

OVERSEAS SERVICE

	FSO**	FSR	FSS	Number	% of Overseas Service
Public Affairs	2	283	97	382	30.5
Administrative	0	30	24	54	4.3
Clerical	0	0	139	139	11.1
Information	0	206	110	316	25.3
Cultural	3	178	102	283	22.6
Engineers and Equip. Tech.	0	3	74	77	6.2
Total				1,251	100.0

* Includes Foreign Service employees assigned to the United States.
** Foreign Service Officers detailed to USIA.

C. AGENCY FOR INTERNATIONAL DEVELOPMENT

1. General Personnel Strength

Table XIII summarizes full-time employment in the Agency for International Development as of June 25, 1962. This table may be summarized as follows:

a. Of the total 15,262 direct-hire employees, the vast majority (12,687) were employed overseas.

b. Approximately 43 per cent (6,544) of the 15,262 employees were United States citizens. Approximately 64 per cent of these 6,544 personnel were in the foreign service, while the remainder were in the departmental service.

155

c. Of the 4,210 United States employees in the foreign service, approximately 9 per cent (241) were located in the United States.

TABLE XIII

AGENCY FOR INTERNATIONAL DEVELOPMENT
Full-time Employment
June 25, 1962*

	All Areas		United States		Overseas	
	No.	%	No.	%	No.	%
Foreign Service Employees	4,210	27.6	241	9.4	3,969**	31.3
Civil Service Employees	2,334	15.3	2,334	90.6	—	—
Total United States Citizen Employment	6,544	42.9	2,575	100.0	3,969	31.3
Foreign National Employees	8,718	57.1	—	—	8,718	68.7
Total Employment	15,262	100.0	2,575	100.0	12,687	100.0

* Excludes 538 employees of other Federal agencies assigned to AID; 274 consultants; and 1,572 employees of contractors.
** Excludes 138 consultants employed overseas.

2. Categories of United States Foreign Service Personnel

Table XIV shows that of the total of 4,210 direct-hire United States foreign service employees more than 80 per cent (3,484) were Foreign Service Reserve Officers, while the remainder were Foreign Service Staff personnel. Tables XV and XVI respectively show a distribution of Foreign Service Reserve Officers and Foreign Service Staff personnel by class.

TABLE XIV

AGENCY FOR INTERNATIONAL DEVELOPMENT
Categories of United States Foreign Service Personnel
June 25, 1962

	Total		United States		Overseas	
	No.	%	No.	%	No.	%
Foreign Service Reserve Officers	3,484	82.8	203	84.2	3,281	82.7
Foreign Service Staff Personnel	726	17.2	38	15.8	688	17.3
Total	4,210	100.0	241	100.0	3,969	100.0

156

TABLE XV

AGENCY FOR INTERNATIONAL DEVELOPMENT
Distribution of Foreign Service Reserve Officers by Class
June 25, 1962

Class	Number	%
L–3*	3	0.1
L–4*	10	0.3
FSR–1	116	3.3
FSR–2	305	8.8
FSR–3	854	24.5
FSR–4	1,006	28.9
FSR–5	743	21.3
FSR–6	332	9.5
FSR–7	101	2.9
FSR–8	14	0.4
Total	3,484	100.0

* Equivalent to classes 3 and 4, respectively, for chiefs of diplomatic mission.

TABLE XVI

AGENCY FOR INTERNATIONAL DEVELOPMENT
Distribution of Foreign Service Staff Personnel by Class
June 25, 1962

Class	Number	%
FSS–1	1	0.1
FSS–2	–	–
FSS–3	1	0.1
FSS–4	1	0.1
FSS–5	3	0.4
FSS–6	5	0.7
FSS–7	3	0.4
FSS–8	9	1.3
FSS–9	42	5.8
FSS–10	88	12.1
FSS–11	198	27.3
FSS–12	325	44.8
FSS–13	50	6.9
Total	726	100.0

3. Categories of Departmental Personnel

Table XVII gives a breakdown of AID departmental personnel by grade.

TABLE XVII

AGENCY FOR INTERNATIONAL DEVELOPMENT
Distribution of Civil Service by Grade
*June 25, 1962 ***

Grade	Number	%
GS–18	13	0.6
GS–17	23	1.0
GS–16	10	0.4
GS–15	217	9.6
GS–14	182	8.0
GS–13	235	10.3
GS–12	115	5.0
GS–11	135	5.9
GS–10	6	0.3
GS–9	182	8.0
GS–8	16	0.7
GS–7	249	11.0
GS–6	209	9.2
GS–5	347	15.3
GS–4	188	8.3
GS–3	111	4.9
GS–2	32	1.4
GS–1	2	0.1
Total	2,272	100.0

* General Schedule and Excepted Schedule employees are combined. Not included in the above figures are Wage Board employees, Excepted Schedule employees whose salaries are above grade 18, and Presidential or "statutory" officials.

4. Functional Distribution of AID Personnel

Tables XVIII and XIX below show a distribution of AID United States citizen foreign service and departmental personnel, respectively, by occupational or functional categories. These data are as of February 28, 1962.

TABLE XVIII

AGENCY FOR INTERNATIONAL DEVELOPMENT
Functional Distribution of Foreign Service Personnel *

February 28, 1962

Category	Number		%	
	FSR	FSS	FSR	FSS
Mission Directors & Deputies	116	–	3.4	–
Program & Economic Officers	261	4	7.6	0.6
Executive Officers & Bus. Man.	208	10	6.1	1.4
Controllers	259	6	7.6	0.9
Personnel Officers & Secy's	43	543	1.2	77.2
Gen'l Services & Records Mgmt.	122	90	3.5	12.8
Mgmt. Analysis Off. & Assts.	2	–	0.1	–
Agriculture	743	2	21.6	0.3
Industry & Mining	233	1	6.8	0.1
Transportation	96	–	2.8	–
Labor	38	–	1.1	–
Health & Sanitation	215	5	6.2	0.7
Education	354	2	10.3	0.3
Public Administration	108	–	3.1	–
Public Safety	131	–	3.8	–
Community Development	47	–	1.4	–
Housing	38	–	1.1	–
Private Enterprise	13	–	0.4	–
Participant Training	85	2	2.5	0.3
Communications Media	86	–	2.5	–
Procurement & Supply	63	2	1.8	0.3
Washington Complement	108	15	3.1	2.1
General & Miscellaneous	69	21	2.0	3.0
Total	3,438	703	100.0	100.0

* Excludes 216 foreign service employees assigned to Washington.

TABLE XIX

AGENCY FOR INTERNATIONAL DEVELOPMENT
Functional Distribution of Civil Service Personnel *

February 28, 1962

Category	Number	%
Social Science	208	9.1
Personnel Admin. & Indust'l Relations	122	5.3
Gen'l Admin., Clerical, Office Service	1,249	54.5
Biological Sciences	17	0.7
Accounting & Budget	231	10.1
Medical & Public Health	18	0.8
Engineering	40	1.7
Legal	34	1.5
Fine & Applied Arts	21	0.9
Business & Industry	84	3.7
Library & Archives	1	0.04
Mathematics & Statistics	29	1.3
Education	24	1.0
Investigation	5	0.2
Supply	53	2.3
Transportation	29	1.3
Wage Board	27	1.2
Miscellaneous	36	1.6
Unknown	64	2.8
Total	2,292	100.0

* Includes 216 foreign service employees assigned to Washington.

APPENDIX C

*Sources of Quotations
Used in Chapter Headings*

Chapter I. JOHN F. KENNEDY: *The State of the Union,* Address of the President of the United States, 87th Cong., 2d Sess., House of Representatives Doc. No. 251, p. 1.

Chapter II. DWIGHT D. EISENHOWER: Annual Budget Message to Congress, Fiscal Year 1956; from *Public Papers of the Presidents: Dwight D. Eisenhower, 1955* (Washington: Government Printing Office, 1955), p. 132.

Chapter III. LOY W. HENDERSON: Commencement Address, Wagner College, Staten Is., N.Y.; in *Congressional Record* (Oct. 6, 1962), p. A7382.

Chapter IV. DEAN RUSK: Remarks before the American Foreign Service Association, Feb. 23, 1961.

Chapter V. THE BROOKINGS INSTITUTION: H. Field Haviland, Jr., *The Formulation and Administration of United States Foreign Policy* (Washington: The Brookings Institution, 1960), p. 19.

Chapter VI. THE WRISTON COMMITTEE: *Toward a Stronger Foreign Service,* Dept. of State Publication 5458 (Washington: Government Printing Office, June 1954), p. 8.

Chapter VII. ALFRED NORTH WHITEHEAD: *The Aims of Education and Other Essays* (New York: The Macmillan Co., 1929), p. 1.

Chapter VIII. ROBERT D. CALKINS: "New Tasks for Our Universities," Address before National University Extension Assoc., Lincoln, Neb., April 30, 1962, p. 7 (mimeo.).

Chapter IX. EUGENE R. BLACK: *The Diplomacy of Economic Development* (Cambridge, Mass.: Harvard University Press, 1960), p. 39.

Chapter X. HENRY M. JACKSON: "Organizing for Survival," *Foreign Affairs* (April 1960), p. 447.